Copyright © 2010 by Aileen Hall
All rights reserved.

Published by
Vantage Point, Inc.
534 East Main Street
Stanville, KY 41659
606.478.9494
http://www.vantagepointads.com
Printed in the United States

All rights reserved. No part of this book may be reproduced or transmitted in any form or by any means. Electronic or mechanical, including photocopying, recording, or by any information storage and retrieval system, without prior written permission from the publisher.

ISBN 978-0-9829820-0-6

Edited by Rhonda Kretzer
    Kitty Baird

Cover and Text Design by Chad Eric Varney

Also by Aileen Hall – *Candlelight*

A Charge for the Angels

"For He shall give His angels charge over you, to keep you in all your ways."
Psalm 91:11 (NKJV)

By Aileen Hall

Dedicated to my daughters,
Nancy and Rhonda, who caused me a few
sleepless nights then repaid me a thousand-fold
with their love and laughter and pure joy in living.

Also to my children's children
– and their children after them –
so long as they want to know about life in
another time and about their own beginnings.

Chapter 1
The world I found

About as far back in the hill country as you can go, in a little town called Banner, Kentucky, a child was born to Jack and Nancy Akers Sellards. The date was December 9, 1926, and to most people, it was just another baby. But I believe God points every child out to His angels, and in this case, He may have said something like, "This one needs a little extra care. She's tough but fragile too, and the world will knock her around. See that it doesn't get the best of her."

I was that child and my belief about that conversation is based on the wonderful care I've been given – far more than anyone has a right to expect.

They named me Mildred Aileen. I never liked the first name, and people always mispronounce the second, the one

The world I found

I'm known by. I had four older siblings: Elsie Naomi, David Estill, Sylvia Juanita, and Edward Graham. They tell me that a few days after I was born, flood waters surrounded our house on Prater Creek where the road turns up Rice Branch. My diapers and gowns had been hung on the line to dry, and Papa had to ride a horse through the water to get them.

Within a few weeks, we moved from that house and rented it to another family. My father had been elected tax commissioner for the county, and he bought another house with sixty acres of property. He was evidently an up-and-coming entrepreneur, well respected in the community, and we were a growing family.

There could have been no better setting for our lives than the new property we moved to. There was a huge orchard with fruit trees – apple, pear, peach, plum and even a quince tree. We had a huge garden and fields to grow strawberries, watermelon, corn, popcorn, and sugar cane for making molasses. There were no restaurants near us, no Wal-Marts, drug stores or beauty shops. We didn't have them, nor did we need them.

Part of the land was hillside where some of the animals grazed, but much of it was playground to us and, when I was old enough, we would spend hours exploring and finding what we thought were treasures – black walnuts, hickory nuts, possum grapes, sassafras roots, tangle-foot greens and wild berries. There were a few wild animals to encounter, such as squirrels, 'possums and a fox now and then, but they were timid and always ran from us. Occasionally there would be a snake, but our dog, Jiggs, took care of that. He always ran a little ahead of us and scouted the area.

The world I found

It's good that our home place was so complete and we had little need to shop, for our roads were unpaved and difficult to travel. My father had a Studebaker, but driving was precarious with many ruts and mud holes, and he had to move slowly, inching his way along. Most people rode horseback or walked wherever they went, and many just stayed home as there was always work to be done. They raised foods and canned them, cared for farm animals and did whatever was required in maintaining households.

Our house was fairly new and one of the nicest in our area. And though there was a garage, barn and many other outbuildings, no thought had been given to inside plumbing. There was a hand-dug well with a framed top and a roped water bucket right beside the back porch. It was supposed to be a real convenience – that we didn't have to carry water farther than that – but no one ever considered piping it into the house.

We had no electricity and, therefore, no refrigeration. Foods were canned, pickled, smoked, dried or cured in whatever methods to keep them safe. There was a concrete building called the cellar that was always cool, and sometimes milk was stored there for a time. On other days it was kept in a nearby spring.

For laundry, there were wash tubs, one for washing clothes on a washboard, and one or two more for rinsing. Each piece of laundry had to be wrung by hand and pinned on a line to dry. Sometimes items that were really soiled, or those our mother thought needed sterilizing, were boiled in a big black pot, also used for making lye soap and rendering lard after a hog was killed.

The world I found

Dave Conn's family was our closest neighbors. Our orchard, a fence and their hay field separated our houses, but we each had a lane that converged on a small bridge that crossed the creek. Our two fields joined in a low spot where the creek sometimes overflowed to create a sand bar. This "beach" was where we built sand castles on summer evenings.

There was a small neighborhood grocery store not far from our house where we bought such things as sugar, flour, salt, soda and baking powder. We didn't need to buy many groceries for we grew most of our foods. About a mile farther down Prater Creek, I. N. Hall had a general store with a larger inventory that included bolts of pretty materials that our mother bought to make dresses, shirts and curtains.

Mr. Hall was also the postmaster, and the Banner post office was located in a corner of his store. He was not very big, a pleasant fellow who wore suspenders, and when I became old enough to observe, his image formed my idea of how a postmaster looked.

The combination store and post office were situated by the railroad tracks, and the train that ran from Ashland to Elkhorn City made a stop there to exchange mail and have passengers get on and off. People expecting mail waited in the store, and Mr. Hall would call off the names as he sorted through the letters and packages. When he announced, "That's all," the group dispersed.

Farther up the creek from us was another post office called Dana. These were the only two located on Prater Creek, a valley of about eight miles, nestled between the mountains. Mail was transported between the two offices by a carrier on horseback and ours was delivered to our roadside mailbox. One of the deliveries my family looked forward to was *The Floyd County Times,* established by Norman Allen the year after I was born. Published in nearby Prestonsburg, the weekly newspaper was our main link to the outside world.

It was my good fortune to have four siblings who were loving and caring, a father who seemed capable of providing well for his family, and the best mother in the whole world. I didn't recognize all its facets right away, but this was the world that welcomed my arrival.

Chapter 2
The Early Years

I was the fifth child, four years younger than Graham, and in the same month I celebrated my second birthday, my baby sister, Vivian Jewel, was born. Elsie's first child, James Kenneth, had arrived three months earlier, and they were at our house a lot. In large families, the big ones helped with the little ones and we never lacked for care.

Our mother took us all to church, and that early exposure made a lasting impression on us. I don't remember a time when I didn't know about God and have an awe of Him. But we were children then and had our own ideas about church that we played out in our make-believe world.

Before I was born, our parents had observed my older siblings having church in our back yard. If a pet or baby chicken died, they held a funeral service. They would sing a while and then ask David to pray. He'd heard some minister praying, "Oh God, we come this evening..." But his version came out, "Oh Dod iss even, Oh Dod." He'd repeat it about three times before saying, "Amen," and they'd sing again.

A few years later, when Jewel and I reached their same ages, we played church too. We didn't think girls should preach, so we mostly sang and shook hands. Then Jewel really got into the church business and started baptizing her dolls. She even cut out paper dolls and submersed them too, but they didn't survive the dip.

I had a special relationship with Aunt Lillie and Uncle Tom and loved being at their house. He was paralyzed from a coal mine accident and confined to a wheelchair for the greater part of his life. There had been no insurance or any form of compensation, and they were as poor as church mice; but they had an abundance of what I enjoyed most – love and affection. Their one child, Evelyn, was seven years older than I, and since there was another baby at our house, I probably wasn't missed too much when I spent time with them.

Their house had the most meager furnishings – a rough table, cane bottom chairs and beds with shuck ticks instead of mattresses – but they always seemed happy and he could make things from nothing. Once he melted a penny and shaped it into a little ring for me, using some colored bead for a set to look like a gemstone. Another time he made a little rocking chair for me and painted it red, and I would sit and rock my dolls. I cherished each doll but bonded especially with a rag doll my mother made, carefully shaping eyes, brows and mouth with colored thread. When I quit playing, I gently tucked it into what I considered a safe place.

The Early Years

Our dogs and cats were considered a part of the family, especially our beloved Jiggs. He was our guardian and companion who roamed the hills with us, killed snakes and fought any animal who posed a threat. We were his charges, and he a most loyal friend.

Jiggs was a bulldog, considered Graham's, but the rest of us came with the package and he guarded us all. Once our family heard dogs fighting in the night but knew Jiggs could hold his own, and he wouldn't allow intruders to his domain. The next morning there was a slick spot worn in a corn field and an intruding dog lay dead. Another time Graham found the seat of a man's pants in the lane near our "hen house." Someone decided to steal some chickens, but both man and beast learned to respect our dog. His timing and instincts were almost perfect for killing a snake, but once a copperhead managed to bite him before it died, and he almost died too. Mama and Graham sat with him before the fireplace all night, cradling his swollen head and treating him with whatever potions she knew to use. They provided intensive care and, against great odds, he recovered.

One animal we didn't love – didn't even like – was Old Fred. My friend Jo Anne asked, "Why does your family keep that mean old bull?" and I said, "I don't know. They keep him in his pen most of the time, but they're always telling us to stay clear of him." I asked David why we had him and he said, "They told me it was for procreation," but I didn't know what that meant and doubt that he did. Sometimes other people brought their cows to see him, and I didn't understand that either.

Sometimes Old Fred was allowed to graze in the well-fenced pasture with the cows, sheep and other animals. Our oak tree with the swing was inside this fence, but the bull was usually at the far end of the field where the grass was greener.

My older siblings seldom invited me when they went out to play with friends, but one day I pleaded and they let me tag along. We went through a gate made of wooden slats with a big latch. I was too little for the swing but it was fun watching them take turns. Then someone yelled, "Here comes Old Fred!" and we saw him running toward us.

There wasn't time to open the gate and three or four were scrambling over the fence. I was almost four and too small to climb, but David lifted me up and tossed me over the gate. He was only twelve and that was difficult, but I guess he had an adrenalin surge. I landed safely in the grass and jumped right up to watch him climb over just ahead of the bull. Old Fred must have gone to procreate somewhere else, as I don't remember seeing him again.

An important part of those early years were the friends who frequented our house and some who lived with us for a time. An old man we called Uncle Jim stayed to help with the farming, and he slept in the room built over the cellar. Once our dad brought a teenager he said was an orphan, and he became a part of the family until Papa caught us playing hide and seek in the barn loft. It was perfectly innocent and I didn't understand why, but soon he was gone and I never heard of him again. When we asked Papa where he was, he just gave some vague answer.

Then a distant cousin, Sam, lived with us many years, and we all loved him. He would bounce us on his knee and sing little ditties like 'Froggie Went a Courtin' and 'Sally in the Garden Siftin' Sand, Susie Upstairs with a Pig-eyed Man.'

The Early Years

We never tired of it or read anything immoral into it. When I got out of bed on cold mornings, Mama would say, "Get your shoes and socks and let Sam put them on you," and I'd go climb in his lap.

A few others, like Malta Akers, became part of our enlarged family and when she accepted Albert Howell's proposal, they were married at our house. She was a real part of the family who helped with whatever needed to be done. We were about four and two when she was giving Jewel and me a bath in a #3 washtub. We were bathed in the same water and, even that young, we argued about which got to go first. Being the baby, Jewel usually won.

Malta had me standing in the tub while she soaped me all over. Papa had spanked me for slipping off to go play with Jo Anne, and my butt was red as fire. She expressed herself freely and kept repeating, "Jack doesn't know how to whip a child. If there's any more spanking done here, I'll be the one to do it." She knew he could hear her, but didn't care.

I sort of forgot she was taking up for me and stuck my tongue out at her. She said, "Do that again," and when I did, she snapped my tongue between two fingers and held it till it burned like fire. I never made that mistake again.

Chapter 3
First Crisis

Springtime was our favorite season, as everything was bursting forth. Fragrant fruit trees were in bloom, farm animals were birthing, and in the evening, frogs were hollering from the creek. Best of all, on the first day of May, we got to go barefoot, a set ritual we always looked forward to. Soon it would be warm enough to wade the creek.

During winter months, the creek froze and became our skating rink, but in summer it was our wading pool, fishing hole and tadpole source. There was the sandbar we called our beach where we made sand castles with our friends next door.

Dave Conn's family made wonderful neighbors. They had a child to match most of our ages, and I paired up with Jo Anne, my first best friend. Our forays at the sandbar usually

First Crisis

ended with our little sisters throwing sand, and we'd have to help them home for our mothers to wash the sand out of their eyes.

A concrete walk ran from our front door to the gate where a gas light burned on summer evenings. We called it our yard light and it lit up a huge area, allowing us to play long and late. Bugs were drawn to the light, and when they fell to the ground, frogs gathered to eat them. It was all fascinating to me.

Graham was nine and I was five when Mama told us a secret. She said, "Maxie had her pups and she's hidden them out somewhere. If you watch where she goes after she eats, I bet you can find them." No toy could have matched the pleasure we got from such discoveries.

It didn't take long to see Maxie go toward the barn, and we were right behind her. We saw the spot where she went under the floor and could hear the pups yipping. Graham crawled in behind her and soon handed me the cutest little brown and white pup.

I was so excited to hold it in my arms while he went back for another. Without looking, I stepped backward onto a board that had a big rusty nail protruding. The nail came all the way through my bare right foot.

Graham scrambled out when he heard me scream. He struggled to free me from the board, and finally hooked his arm under my leg and jerked me free.

I left a trail of blood from the barn to the house where Mama and Sylvia did what they knew to do. They washed my foot in antiseptics and bandaged it in clean white strips of cloth. Mama told me I couldn't play for the rest of the day and she found my doll to lie with me in the porch swing.

First Crisis

There were four pups in Maxie's litter and Graham brought them, one by one, for me to see. As we looked them over, we decided on a name for each one.

With all they had done to "doctor" me, I thought I would be better by the next day, but my foot hurt and started to swell. With each day it seemed to worsen, and red streaks formed around my ankle.

Someone went to get Dr. Martin, who lived about five miles away. He suggested they try poultices to draw the poison out, and a series of different ones were tried. One treatment involved burning wool and holding my foot directly over the smoke. It smelled awful. Then beet leaves were crushed into a poultice to wear under the bandage.

Mama boiled a bed sheet in the big black pot she used to make soap and cut it into strips for a supply of clean bandages. Within a week, I couldn't walk at all and had to be carried wherever I went. Sometimes I'd cry in the night, and Mama would come to give me a drink and sit with me till I was sleeping again. At other times, I was awakened as she lifted the cover to see if the redness had spread.

Just when my care was demanding so much of the family, trouble came in another form. Elsie's husband died suddenly of a ruptured appendix. I was too young to understand the tragedy it meant for her. She had Kenneth, who was three, and was expecting her second child. It was an inconsolable grief, and even with me hurting, Mama had to support and care for her, too.

The funeral was on a Friday and, afterwards, Dr. Martin came by our house to check my foot. I didn't understand all the words they used, but red streaks had gone to my knee, and

First Crisis

the foot had swollen to more than twice its normal size. I heard the doctor say, "We'll do it Monday," and I completely trusted them to make me well. I saw Mama wipe her eye. She cried a lot since Jim died.

Aside from the soreness and pain, I rather enjoyed the attention. When a fresh bandage was in place, David was there to lift me up. He said, "Sylvia is popping corn and you don't want to miss it." He sat me on a cabinet where I could see her shake the cooker over the burner and listen to the corn pop and bounce against the lid. It sounded like a thousand little firecrackers and I always liked that.

As she poured the popcorn into a pan, I asked, "Sylvia, what is amputate?"

She looked startled for a minute and finally mumbled, "How would I know?"

Two days later, on Sunday morning, a politician came to see Papa and they were having breakfast in the dining room. I was propped in a chair in the kitchen, curious to know what they were talking about. I'd found several conversations lately were about me, so I eased out of my chair and hopped over by the door to listen. Their coffee cups were emptied and, going to the kitchen for more, Papa looked back, talking to his guest, and didn't see me. His full weight stepped directly on my foot. Even through the heavy bandage, blood shot all the way across the room and splattered the opposite wall.

"I've killed my baby!" he cried. He grabbed me up and ran to the porch. His guest hurried to get Dr. Martin while blood kept pouring onto the ground. There was such a puddle it seemed none would be left, but it finally stopped.

Dr. Martin kept checking my pulse and breathing and, before leaving, said to Mama, "Nancy, I know this accident

First Crisis

has scared you half to death. We'll postpone the surgery and I'll be back to check on her tomorrow." I later learned I had been scheduled for amputation the following day.

When I awoke next morning, the redness and swelling were gone, leaving only a soreness where the skin had burst. Though with a limp, I was able to walk to the table for breakfast. I didn't have to be carried anymore, and soon I was running and playing again.

Many years passed before I understood that the road mapped for me required both feet, and what seemed so drastic to us that day was no accident at all.

Chapter 4
Growing Pains

I was never a robust child and the ordeal with the foot had taken something out of me. Mama was always reminding me, "You didn't drink all your milk." Sometimes she'd say, "I made potatoes just the way you like them, and surely you can finish what's on your plate." I couldn't gain an ounce, but I was still a bundle of energy.

I had looked forward to starting school in July of 1932. (Rural schools ran from July through January.) I wouldn't be six until December, but she and my teachers agreed I was ready, and I enrolled in Banner Grade School.

I loved going to school, and especially that I could stop off at Aunt Lillie's afterward. Mama knew I loved going there and allowed it for a time. When she sent Graham to get me, she also sent them milk, butter and eggs. But one day she told me Aunt Lillie was sick and I had to come directly home till she was better. The only exception was that, in case of rain, I could still go. That caused me to wish for rain every day. One afternoon it looked cloudy, but I held my arm out and felt nothing. I sauntered toward home and was almost there when I felt a sprinkle and ran all the way back to her house.

She took me in her lap and asked, "Where have you been? The other children passed a good while ago." I just said I was going home and it started to rain. She started asking how far I got and I wouldn't tell. She asked, "Did you get to Rhodes Meade's?" and I shook my head no. "Did you get to Will Hurd's?" and again I nodded no. Then she asked, "Did you get to Bob Boyd's?" And when I said, "Yes," she doubled over in laughter, for I was almost home.

Sylvia did much of the housework, though she was only twelve. I knew Mama wasn't feeling well, but in my innocence I didn't understand why. Dr. Martin was there one evening and he and Papa walked out to look at the cattle. I went to bed that August night thinking he might have come to buy a calf, but the next morning I learned I had a new baby brother. They named him Jack Buford.

I was quiet and shy around strangers; Jewel was the unpredictable one who never saw a stranger. She would ask, "What's your name? Where you live? You got any children?" As sure as Mama told her not to tell something, she would blurt it out and embarrass her. She was just two years younger than I and, for a long time, we were packaged as "the girls." We slept together and would sometimes fight, so we'd lay a pillow or draw an imaginary line between us and dare each other to cross over.

A common refrain around our house was, "Send the girls to gather the eggs," or "Give the girls a bath." Jewel was the only family member I fought with, probably because we were packaged so closely.

Becky was a neighbor who was hired to help with the laundry, canning and other work. She liked us all, but especially Graham, whose name she always mispronounced. Sylvia later wrote a poem about him and described how Becky would clasp her hands and say, "God bless that little Grem!"

Any news that happened beyond Prater Creek was slow to reach us, however, a local event in 1933, made national news. There was a school board election going on at Dana that had factions with deep feelings about the outcome. When someone objected to a decision, another pulled a gun. Quite quickly, two men lay dead and nine others were wounded. Three died the following day. I was six years old and, from our front porch, we could see the hearses and ambulances make their way up the rough road to get them. Though I knew none of them, one of those killed would be the great-grandfather of my children.

We also watched other people who passed up and down that road. There was a family we knew as Ghent and Marth and their little dog Mikey. They didn't have a car or a horse and walked to and from the store. Ghent would be in front with Marth about six feet behind him, and little Mikey about six feet behind her. We thought it was funny that they never walked side by side, and Graham and I would call to each other, "Hey, come and look! Here comes Ghent and Marth and little Mikey." Our delight in such simple things is proof that it didn't take much to amuse us.

Jewel and I were about five and seven and still taking our baths in a washtub. It was summertime and Mama had moved the tub into the cellar where it didn't matter if we splattered water onto the concrete floor.

Sylvia filled the tub with water, laid out the soap and towels and called for us to come take a bath. Jewel and I raced to see who could get there first and I won, peeled off my clothes and jumped in the water. Feeling spiteful, Jewel slammed the door shut, but I was still jubilant about being first as I lathered up. The room was dark except for the light coming in under the door. As my eyes adjusted, I thought I saw something move. A snake was crawling under the door and coming right toward me!

I was deathly afraid of snakes and Sylvia heard my blood curdling scream. She came running and saw the snake partly through the door, grabbed a nearby hoe and whacked it in two. When she opened the door to tell me I was safe, I shot out of the tub and ran outside, still screaming and jumping up and down. Every family member within earshot came running. With everybody looking, Jewel smirked and said, "I think you need your towel." That's when it hit me that I was as naked as a jaybird, and I started bawling all over again. I was probably the most modest member of the family and thought I might die right there. Not only my father and brothers saw me, but the neighbors across the road were straining to see what was happening. Mama was wearing an apron and I tried to cover myself with it, but it was too short. Finally Sylvia tossed me a towel, but I couldn't quit sobbing.

Mama put her arm around me and kept repeating, "Calm down! It's all right. See, the snake is dead." I glanced over where it lay, now in three pieces, but by the way I felt right then, its chance of recovery was better than mine.

Chapter 5
The Home Place

We should have given a name to the first home I remember. It had almost everything for independent living if you were willing to work. If you weren't interested in one facet of your surroundings, there were a thousand others to enjoy.

The major tasks in running the place were done by our parents and older siblings. I had no idea how much effort it took on our mother's part to keep us all clothed and fed and see that our recreation was wholesome. Papa didn't get close to us the way she did. He saw to the livestock and to planting and harvesting of everything but Mama's garden, but he seemed to think his was the scolding role when we'd done something amiss. We just naturally went to Mama with our personal interests. She was pretty lenient about what we could do when we weren't in school and not yet old enough for things like cooking, canning or quilting. We had plenty of time to play in the creek or scramble over the hills and she always knew who our playmates were.

As soon as I was big enough to reach the dishpan on a table, I was taught to wash dishes. Most of my chores were pretty simple, like making the beds and sweeping the porch and on wash day, I carried water to help fill the tubs and then carried wet laundry to hang on the line.

During spring planting, Papa took my bothers and two or three "work hands" to the fields for planting corn. One of my jobs was to go call them in for dinner. As soon as they heard me yell, "Dinner's ready!" they immediately stopped work and headed for the house.

One day I ran all the way to the field and asked Graham if I could ride one of the mules back to the barn. He was only ten, but he handled the mules. He helped me climb on Barney's back and led him by a strap so he wouldn't run with me. It was just the back of a mule, but I felt like I was on top of the world. Why hadn't I thought of this before? I would do it again tomorrow.

The mules were accustomed to veering by the creek for a drink, and today was no different – we headed that way. Most of the creek was shallow, but there was a little curve where the water formed a pool to make an ideal drinking spot. When Barney bent down to drink, his whole body tilted. With absolutely nothing to hold to, I pitched head-first over his back, down his neck, between his ears and right into the water.

When Graham pulled me out, I was crying and spluttering, but I was little and limber and not hurt at all. It was hard to keep up the good cry I deserved with Graham laughing so hard. In fact, I don't think I've ever seen him laugh so hard. Even Barney turned to stare. Just seeing me slide headfirst between Barney's ears must have made his day. By the time I'd changed my clothes, I'd also changed my mind. I didn't ever want to ride a mule again.

I helped feed the livestock and it seemed only natural that I learned to milk the cows. They let me start with a cow known to be gentle, but as I sat on a stool, pumping milk into a bucket, I sometimes got swished by her tail. That was her defense if a bug landed on her back or she just felt like scratching, but my head got in the way of her target. Some cows might kick at you or kick the bucket, but mine was more docile.

Another chore that was my responsibility just happened now and then, always at an inconvenient time. Either we had just sat down to eat, or I was on third base and ready to score in a game of round town, when someone discovered the sheep were in the strawberry patch. Whatever I was doing came to a halt, for I had to run. Sheep could clean a field like a sweeper on a carpet. They ate berries, plants and all. I learned to take Jiggs with me, and he made short work of getting them out. He was no bigger than a small sheep, and he would bite himself before he'd nip one of them, but they didn't know that. He made them believe he'd swallow them whole. They rushed back to their own lot, going all the way to the back side. It was funny to watch them, but when the job was over, my ball game was over too, or supper was cold.

There was never a shortage of chickens or eggs at our place – they were everywhere. Hens have a natural instinct for nesting, and that's how many families raise chickens. It isn't unusual for a hen to hide her nest, lay the eggs and sit on them until they've hatched. Then she marches out with her new little family.

That might have happened once in a while at our place, but we had incubators that hatched eggs, 100 at a time. When one hatching was done, the trays were set over again. The baby chicks, called biddies, were moved to a brooder house, equipped with a canopy warmed by an electric light. When they grew into pullets, they were transferred to the hen house or a lot.

When the brooder house was finally vacated, we were allowed to use it as a playhouse until hatching time again. Neighboring children joined us and we made a big deal of cleaning and making ready, scrubbing away any possibility of chicken mites with brooms, water, and lye soap. Then we gathered loose objects to be our make-believe furniture and, when we got it pretty much to our liking, we took our dolls to their new home.

Free gas came with our property, and that was great for heating and cooking and for that wonderful "yard light" that made it possible to play long after dark. Papa bought a Delco generator plant from Henry Porter, so another convenience we had was electric lights. We had no appliances, but lights dangled on cords from our ceilings.

Papa had the only mill on the creek for grinding corn into meal after it had been harvested and dried, and one day a week was spent in that process. Neighbors brought their corn to be ground, and they paid for the service with a portion of their meal. We had to buy flour at the store but, like so much else we ate, our corn meal was home grown. Care had been taken to put the mill in an open spot, a good distance from the pigpen. Pigs liked to play dirty and make a mud hole to "waller" in.

Besides the two mules, we had cows, sheep, pigs, chickens, ducks, geese, dogs and cats – and all of these had a definite reason for being there. Mama picked feathers from the ducks and geese to make pillows. The mules pulled the plows to till the soil and the cats, considered pets, kept the buildings rodent free.

The sheep that invaded our strawberry patch were valuable and had to be nurtured, and many times we had to rescue a lamb, abandoned and left in the cold. We kept it wrapped in a blanket in a box by the fire, feeding it warm milk from a baby doll's bottle. A lamb was the sweetest animal and we took great pleasure in caring for one.

The main purpose of the sheep, though, was their wool, and every spring there was a "sheep shearing" that was quite an operation. As children, we had a natural curiosity about anything going on and were allowed to watch from the barn loft or a safe vantage point. The full grown sheep had to be tied and restrained on tables while the wool was sheared from their backs. It didn't hurt them, but they rebelled and made it difficult. The wool was then packed into large bags and shipped off by train to be returned within weeks in the form of warm blankets. Some were sold to neighbors as we had a surplus, and no other family on the creek raised sheep.

As soon as weather turned cold enough with the beginning of winter, a "hog killing" was an expected ritual. A frame was built, sturdy enough to support a 400 pound hog. A neighbor or relative usually helped clean and dress the hog and was given a portion of the meat. Slabs of bacon were treated with salt, hams were hung in the smokehouse to cure, sausage was made and stored in the cloth tubing Mama made for it, and the fat was rendered into lard for cooking.

The Home Place

We were familiar with almost every inch of our surroundings, especially our playground in the hills. We found level spots for an imaginary playhouse and covered small logs or rocks with soft green moss to be our furniture.

Once, we spent hours making a new play area just right before leaving it for the night. We returned the next day to find a long black snake draped across our couch. You never saw such scurrying to get off that hill. We gave up on that playhouse but never lost heart about making another. We just had to remember to take Jiggs along next time.

We loved the cave that sheltered us from the wind and rain, and the huge grapevine we could hold onto and swing over a ravine when we had our courage up. Sometimes we packed a lunch but, if we didn't, there were nuts and wild berries to satisfy us. Many times we climbed to the very top of the hill to look down the other side at the bigger valley where the railroad tracks and Big Sandy River lay side-by-side. We watched the cars moving on the two-lane road that runs north and south, and I wondered what lay beyond the horizons. We also looked down on U. S. Rt. 23, the road that goes from Michigan to Florida and intersects with all other roads, but we had little thought of ever traveling it.

Our house sat at the base of the hill, and the gentle stream called Prater Creek wound through the property, marking off cornfields and melon patches. Every season had its own special crop to plant or reap, its own birthing rituals and its times for sitting on the porch listening to Mother Maybelle Carter sing songs like "Wildwood Flower" and "Little Brown Jug" on our crank-style Victrola phonograph.

I've never heard of another home place quite like it, and I treasure the memories.

Chapter 6
Good Times, Mostly

Our home was a happy place with music ringing from the rafters. Sylvia could make our Hammond organ fairly dance and Graham and David both played guitar and banjo. Even Papa picked up a banjo every now and then. Neighbors loved to gather at our house to make music. My brothers' friends, Lum, Ike and Chalmer, brought fiddles and other instruments along to fill out the band and they all sang in beautiful harmonies. What difference did it make that none had formal training? What we had was the best we'd ever heard. It must have appealed to others too because the boys and their friends eventually got a contract for a live radio show on a station in Williamson, West Virginia.

On summer evenings they made music from our front porch, and we younger kids played games by the gas light at the end of the walk. We played hopscotch, marbles, tag, and antney over, where we threw a ball over an outbuilding for someone on the other side to catch. Sometimes we caught lightning bugs and put them in a jar. In bad weather, we played inside games called fruit basket, poor old puss, and hide and seek. We hid in closets, under the beds and behind doors. Just being together was fun and we often squealed in laughter. Sometimes Papa, absorbed in a newspaper, would call out, "Children! Children! Quieten down!" But Mama always countered, "Leave them alone, Jack. They're just children once."

Our mother really made our house a home. She was a wonderful cook and, when company came, she could dress a hen and have a feast on the table in no time. Uncle Floyd and Aunt Rhoda came often and we were delighted to see them. She was a delicate, soft-spoken little woman who brought us beautiful hand-stitched quilts and aprons. He was big and boisterous and more fun than any man we'd ever known. He took my brothers froggin' in the creek and teased and played with all of us. He gave us nickels and dimes if we promised to be Democrats. I giggled and hugged him and took his money but it was his attention I really enjoyed.

Their home in Ashland was the one place we enjoyed going as a family. They took us to Armco Park and I was fascinated by the squirrels that scurried about. The ones at home seemed to know about hunters and would never run in the open like that. I never understood how squirrels knew when to be afraid.

Franklin Delano Roosevelt was now in his third year as President and people often commented about being glad that "Hoover times" were over. The great depression that had begun in President Hoover's first term was by no means over, but the outlook seemed to be improving.

It had been a long time since our family bought anything new and we were all excited when the decision was made to buy a radio. It was a Silvertone brand, a beautiful console model that we ordered from the Sears, Roebuck & Co. catalog. It was shipped by train to our nearest railway station at Allen, more than three miles from our home. As soon as we heard it had arrived at the depot, David and Graham hitched the mules, Barney and Ellen, to a big sled padded with straw. When they headed out to bring it home, we were so jubilant you'd have thought it was Christmas time.

The radio was a big deal to our music loving bunch and the same big generator that powered our lights made it possible for us to enjoy it. On Saturday nights, our house overflowed with young people who came to listen to the Grand Ole Opry. We always had at least two dishpans full of home grown popcorn ready to serve by the time announcer George D. Hay, dubbed the Solemn Old Judge, was tuned in on WSM Radio out of Nashville, Tennessee. When the popcorn ran out, as it always did, we just popped more. We had no soda pop then so we all drank water from a bucket using a common dipper made from a gourd.

Some of the Opry stars we enjoyed were Uncle Dave Macon, the Fruit Jar Drinkers, Possum Hunters and Gully Jumpers. The show was lively to say the least, but any concern that it might be un-Christian was put to rest when Roy Acuff sang "The Great Speckled Bird."

Other entertainment was where we found it. In one of David's high school classes, he learned that chickens sometimes died from food stuck in their craws. Having learned this, he felt obliged to help a hen he saw drooping around. He caught her and tied her to a board. Then he operated, washed out her craw, and sewed her up. Soon she was running around the lot again and teasing the roosters.

Good Times, Mostly

David performed several more operations when he suspected others of the flock were ailing. If a chicken could be smart, it would be wise to walk with a spring in its step when he was in the vicinity. Once he and one of his buddies shared some beer with a hen. She liked it well enough, and sipped it often enough, that she staggered around the chicken lot. They laughed so hard the rest of us ran to see what was happening.

We had a lot of freedom to roam and play, oblivious to any danger in our familiar world. One Sunday when I was about nine, my friend Mary Louise came to spend the day. I was wearing a new blue dress Mama had just made for me and felt very dressed up. We often went exploring when we got together. This time we'd had a pouring rain and the creek was overflowing with backwater rising in the lower fields, so we decided to go see how high the water was.

We found David and his friend, Lum, floating around on a raft they had built from some old boards. They offered to take us for a ride and we climbed right on. We were having great fun but suddenly the raft got caught in a swirl of swift water and swung around under a tree. I was caught in the path of a big limb that swooped me right into the muddy water. None of us could swim, and I disappeared beneath the dark water. David shouted to Lum, "Grab that limb and hold on!" Then he laid flat on his stomach, stretched out his arms and felt for me. Evidently I came up beneath the raft and couldn't be seen, but a shoeless foot floated out and he grabbed it. It slipped from his hand, but he had pulled me from under the raft and was able to catch a strand of my long hair. With Mary Louise sobbing and Lum clinging desperately to the limb, David grabbed my arms, lifted me out and laid me face down on the raft. I had gulped the muddy water until my lungs and stomach were filled. They could see I wasn't breathing. Frantically, David lifted me from the hips. Water gushed out, and I gasped for air. Lum maneuvered the raft to dry ground and Mary Louise jumped off and went running home to tell her folks what happened.

David and Lum managed to get me home. I was cold and wet, shaking all over, and my teeth chattered. Soon Mama had me enfolded in one of those warm wool blankets we called our sheep blankets since they came from our own flock.

I was crying and still scared as I heard David telling Mama what happened. His words rushed like the current, "The water was so muddy we couldn't see her anywhere but she came up right under the raft and her foot popped up almost in my hand!" He described the details about grasping my hair and how I wasn't breathing and how he first thought I was dead. He was practically in shock himself having almost lost the little sister who adored him.

As they talked, I became aware of Sylvia filling a wash tub with warm water. When I recovered enough, she scrubbed me from head to toe removing every trace of mud. Had it been possible, she would have turned me inside out to get it all. My pretty new dress lay crumpled on the floor looking very much like a rag mop, and Jewel was running in circles rattling on about how we had no business on that old raft anyway, urging Sylvia to hurry so we could go play.

But play was the farthest thing from my mind. I only wanted to be close to Mama. I lay with my head resting on her lap – the safest place I knew – and fell asleep. As I slept, cozy and warm, I have an idea the angels were asking, "Lord, what next with this child?"

Chapter 7
Brand New Shoes

We didn't have many extracurricular activities in grade school, but we did have a 4-H club led by Sam Isbell, our Floyd County Extension agent. He made regular visits, and one day he said he wanted us to be involved in competition with the other schools at the upcoming county fair. My teacher, Miss Allen, suggested he take a look at my handwriting. I was in sixth grade and wrote Lincoln's Gettysburg Address for him to see.

I saw him smile at her when he picked it up and placed it carefully in a folder. Before leaving, he came by my desk and said, "I'm really pleased with your writing." It was nice to be complimented on something so simple. I didn't get to go to the fair to see my entry on display but, when it ended, Mr. Isbell brought it back with a big blue ribbon attached. It had won First Place Penmanship. He made a big deal of presenting it to me, and it was the talk of our school for a while.

 I loved books and the stories that almost always began, "Once upon a time..." When we studied Robert Louis Stevenson's book, <u>A Child's Garden of Verses</u>, I especially loved his poem, *The Land of Counterpane*. Miss Allen assigned us a report on the life of the author and I found out he had died in 1894. He'd been dead all those years, and yet his words were still warm and vibrant. I imagined how great it would be to write a book and have something that would last longer than I did.

 Our school was built up on concrete posts, probably in case of flooding, and we played games under the floor. We also had a ball field where we played a game called "round town." Ellen Jones and I were good athletes, considered tomboys then, and we could hit the ball well and outrun most of the boys. The team captains got to choose their teams for each game. One always picked Ellen and the other chose me. We never got to play on the same side, for we balanced out the chances of winning by being separated.

 Once during school vacation, there was a round town game in the making but Jewel and I had to wash the dinner dishes before we could play. Mama had a rule: the dishes had to be rinsed in scalding water. We'd been taught how to heat the water in a tea kettle and pour it over the dishes, but that took time and we were in a hurry to join the game so we decided to take a shortcut. It wasn't long before we announced, "We're finished!" Mama said, "You can't be finished this soon," but we answered, "Come look."

 She came into the kitchen to find the kitchen clean with the dishes put away neatly in the cabinet. But then she asked, "Did you scald them?" We didn't dare lie, so I said, "No. But we washed and rinsed them real good."

Brand New Shoes

She walked over to the 100 piece dinner set in the china cabinet and asked us to show her exactly which ones had been scalded and which ones hadn't. We tried to remember how many plates, bowls and cups we had washed. When I guessed "Eight plates," Jewel argued, "No, I think it was nine."

"Since we don't know for sure," Mama said, "you'll just have to scald them all." It was a good lesson for us but we missed that game altogether.

By now I was ten and becoming more interested in my appearance and choosing my own clothes. I'd become a little embarrassed by my shoes ever since I'd seen a prettier style in a catalog. I showed them to Papa. "These are the ones I want," I told him. He barely looked at the picture but focused on the shoes I was wearing. "Do yours still fit?" he asked. When I admitted they did, he said they were still sturdy and I didn't need new shoes. We never had more than one pair at a time.

Not to be discouraged, I put my shoes through a rough time. I drug the toes over rocks and splashed through puddles, shamelessly abusing them with every opportunity. After a couple weeks I went back to Papa proudly wearing my shabby shoes. "My shoes are worn out, Papa," I said. "I need these." I showed him again the pretty slippers in the catalog, wrote my size in the corner, then carefully tore the worn page out and folded it neatly for him. "All right," he said, and put it in his pocket.

The day finally came when he would bring them home. I saw the old Studebaker coming up the road and ran to meet him in the lane. I'd never been this excited about any clothing item and was fairly bubbling when he handed me the package.

Brand New Shoes

When I opened the box, I burst into tears. Inside was the ugliest pair of boy's shoes I'd ever seen, no kin to the pretty slippers I'd asked for. They were rough, raw-looking leather that laced above my ankles. "But you promised!" I wailed. His only comment was, "You're too rough on shoes. I had to get you some that would last."

I wished I'd taken better care of my old ones, for I liked them much better. I was so humiliated in wearing the new ones to school that I sat with my feet pulled up under the desk in class and didn't join the others on the playground during recess. The other students must have wondered what was wrong with me, for most of them wore rough shoes too and didn't even notice. But this was a real disappointment that would take some time to get over.

Chapter 8
A Close Call

I truly hated those ugly shoes but they were so sturdy I couldn't wear them out. I could have waded the creek in them and it wouldn't hurt. They had coarse laces and a little steel tap on the back of each heel – a far cry from the dainty slippers I wanted.

We had little grade school sweethearts which meant little more than smiles across the room, and a few times some boy had written a note to say, "I love you better than a cat loves cream." Not very eloquent but just being noticed was exciting, and now I was sure no one would even look at me with those grubby looking feet. Sometimes a boy shyly asked if he could carry my books as we walked from school, which both pleased and embarrassed me. Someone was sure to tell and I'd be teased at home with, "I hear So-and-So is sweet on you." I never liked being teased that way.

There was no sex education except for what school girls whispered about, and that wasn't enough to understand any of it. My innocence was rare for even then, for I was five when my baby brother was born and he was a total surprise. It

A Close Call

wasn't that I had no curiosity at all – there were just too many other things to claim my interest. At the age of eleven, I was still a tomboy who enjoyed climbing trees and fishing in the creek. I liked competing with my brothers, nephews and the boys at school.

Mama insisted I stay with Elsie, especially at night. She was a widow with two little boys, and I was the most likely one to be some company to them. Our houses were a mile and a half apart and I always walked the distance. I traveled it so much I could almost go blindfolded.

Preacher Stratton's house sat beside the road and I passed it coming and going. Many times he was working outside and walked to the gate to meet me and ask about my family and how I was doing. He was known over the state as The Little Shepherd of the Hills, and he made me feel special. After a brief visit, he always patted my shoulder and said, "Bless your heart, child," and I felt I carried his special blessing with me. Some preachers I knew had a disapproving look, but I knew Preacher Stratton cared about me, and I loved him dearly.

One excitement I had at my sister's house was seeing the Banner bridge being built and knowing we would not have to travel the old county road anymore. I'd never seen construction work done where they used giant cranes and heavy equipment. We watched as they poured the huge footers and hoisted the heavy cables to support a swinging bridge. We could see the men working from the front porch, and when they left for the day, we'd go take a closer look at what they'd done.

I never really disliked staying with Elsie, but she had rules we didn't have at home. She allowed us to eat only at meal time and it seemed like she was forever telling us to wash our hands. We had to wash so much I thought we might take the hide off. There was probably so much work going on at home that no one had time for rules like that. We had more freedom to eat or not eat, wash or not wash, so long as we did our chores and took regular baths.

Those ugly shoes were still an embarrassment, and it's a pity I detested them so, for they became a life saving factor in my most frightful experience as a child. I'd gone home from Elsie's, knowing I had to return for the night. There was a ball game going and I didn't want to leave, but Mama kept coaxing me to get started before dark. I waited too long and darkness was falling when I headed out. I'd walked that road a thousand times and knew every curve, every obstacle, every sound, but suddenly I heard something different. They were footsteps, rapid and strong. I glanced back and saw the form of a man following me.

I picked up my pace, and so did he, but his legs were so much longer and he was gaining on me. I felt fear gripping me and sensed real danger. I broke into a run but the sound of his feet told me he was running too. The whole road was deserted and he caught me just where it started a downward slope. He looped his long right arm around my neck, stopping me in my tracks with my back against him.

I recognized him as a neighbor who lived by the railroad tracks with his parents and younger brother. I knew who he was, but had never encountered him in any way. He was about twenty, I was eleven, and I'd never heard the word he used in telling me what he was going to do. His arms around me were so strong they felt like a vise, and there was no way I could break that grip. By standing on my left leg, my right foot was

A Close Call

free and I drew it forward to kick backward with all the strength in my body.

I had no idea I could kick so hard, but the steel tap on my shoe nailed his shin with such impact that he doubled over in pain, releasing me as he fell. I heard him mutter, "You little bitch!" He might have said some other things too – but I was gone. I could outrun most of the boys on my ball team, and now it seemed as if my feet were on fire. I sailed right by Preacher Stratton's place, across the railroad tracks, past I. N. Hall's store and on to Elsie's house where I collapsed like a sack thrown on her front steps.

She left Julian crying to come and ask what was the matter with me and, still out of breath, I just said, "I ran." I had my back to her and she couldn't see the tears running down my face. She seemed to be stymied, but I never told her what happened. I just sat there a very long time. Somehow I believed it would be my own fault if I got hurt, and I would have fought as long as I had breath. But determined as I was, I was no match for him. He was almost twice my age and more than twice my size. Had the assault continued, I doubt I would be here to write the story.

But there was a Presence on that dark road that neither of us could see – guiding my foot with the little steel tap and giving me strength to land that kick.

Chapter 9
Transition

My assailant probably expected me to report the close call, for he and his family disappeared from the local landscape. I don't remember ever seeing any of them again. But now I knew to be wary, and it was a step toward growing up.

Our home place was much like Eden to us, and life was happy. There was always work to be done, but the crops flourished and there was a never-ending display of nature to observe. From the farm animals to our adventures in the hills, there was always something new and interesting to discover.

I didn't sense the undercurrent when I first heard Sylvia say, "Mama, I wish you wouldn't worry so." And one day I overheard Papa say sharply to Graham, "Money doesn't grow on trees." Sylvia replied, "No it doesn't. And trees wouldn't drink it up."

By this time, Elsie and David were already married with families of their own, so Sylvia and Graham were the two oldest at home. When Graham dropped out of high school to join the CCC's (Civilian Conservation Corps), I thought it was just something he wanted to do. I later learned it was a way to earn money to send home for us. He never mentioned – then or ever – that he made any sacrifice, but he was so young for such responsibilities.

When Jewel was five, she found out the Fourth of July celebration was coming to nearby Prestonsburg. There would be fireworks and a carnival atmosphere, and Jewel begged to go with Papa to "see the Fourth." Mama was apprehensive but Jewel pleaded and Papa agreed to take her. Mama reluctantly allowed her to go, telling Sylvia, "Surely, if he has his baby with him, he'll look after her."

There were a lot of people milling around, and Papa went into a place to have a drink with a buddy. He told Jewel to wait for him but he didn't come back. Hours passed and one of our neighbors, Malta Crum, saw Jewel wandering around alone and frightened in the crowd. "Have you seen my daddy?" Jewel asked. Malta took her home with her for the night and brought her on to our house the next morning. Mama had stayed awake all night, waiting, watching and praying for them to come home safely.

Sylvia and Graham shared the worries and always knew when things weren't right, but Mama never allowed any of us to be critical. And certainly no failing on Papa's part was to be an excuse for any character flaw of our own. Once he came home late and slept in the next morning after the rest of us were up and busy. When he did get up, she asked me to go make his bed.

A ten dollar bill had been dropped on the floor by the bed. Accustomed to dealing in nickels and dimes, it looked like a lot of money to me. I stuck it in my pocket and ran to the kitchen whispering "Mama, look! Look what I found!"

When I told her where I'd found it she softly replied, "You know that doesn't belong to you, so take it back to your dad."

"But Sylvia says he wastes money. Why give it to him?"

"That's not your concern," she told me. "It's what you do that you have to live with, so give it back now." It was a lesson I'd never forget.

Much of Papa's work as tax commissioner was done at our house by Sylvia and David. From the time I was in fifth grade, I came home after school to be given a stack of forms with family names and statistics and told to separate them alphabetically. I got them ready for Sylvia and David to transfer the information to big record books. That's how I learned that I truly enjoyed working.

People over the county liked Papa and praised his fairness in tax assessments, but word of his drinking got around and he lost the next election. I didn't know about mortgage payments or that ours was behind. While most working people are paid regular wages, he was paid for the work when he completed all the records, and the bank gave him extra time to catch up on late payments.

When the work was completed and he went for his pay, he didn't come home again for days. When he finally showed up, the money was gone – and that meant our property was gone too. Within a few months we moved back to the rent house, a traumatic experience for Mama and Sylvia, but they went about shaping up the place and saying very little.

I would soon be going to high school and was excited about that. I would have a half mile less to walk each day to catch the school bus, and now we lived just across the road from Aunt Lillie. Our beloved hills and grounds were still there, and I guess I thought we could always go back if we wished, but the others knew better.

Our move meant giving up the orchards, strawberry patch, bee hives, grape arbors and the larger garden spot. It also meant the loss of free gas we had to heat the house and cook with, and the popular gas light that lit up the whole area. We would now have to burn coal for heating and cooking.

Orville Jones was my teacher in both seventh and eighth grades, and I thought he was the greatest. Our school year ended in January, and the only fanfare we had was a few kind words with our diplomas. Mr. Jones knew I was anxious to begin high school and encouraged me to enroll for the second semester just beginning at Betsy Layne. This seemed ideal, so I hardly missed a day between elementary and high school.

Riding the school bus was another experience. We had a swinging bridge across the Big Sandy River and drivers weren't allowed to take the bus over it, so I had to walk a mile and cross the bridge to the bus stop. Our Prater Creek road wasn't paved and was muddy much of the time, so the walk wasn't too easy. But there were others to walk with and we didn't consider it difficult. It was just a part of going to school.

It seemed something new was happening every day. In one of my very first classes, a paper wad came sailing across the room and hit me in the head. I turned just in time to see Walter Hall drop his arm.

Chapter 10
The Saddest Time

Classmate Mary Williams still remembers my first day of high school. "You had the look of a little lost puppy," she says, and that's exactly how I felt. It was the beginning of a new semester and all the others were well acquainted, while I was a total stranger. But it takes only one friend to make you feel welcome and, by the end of the first week, I had settled in. The shy little girl from Prater Creek had become one of the bunch.

Glee Club was great and, though I didn't have a solo voice, it blended well with others. When asked to provide music for some program or service, Miss Hale took me along, and it was fun going anywhere with the group.

I still stayed with Elsie much of the time, and though I preferred the atmosphere of home, it was nice not having to walk that mile to catch the bus so early in the morning. It was a very short distance to cross the bridge from her house.

The Saddest Time

I became friends with her sister-in-law, Ruth, who was older than I and worked in her father's store. I enjoyed hanging out with her and soon found myself helping with the work. I stocked shelves, ran errands and helped wait on customers. She was glad to have me do it, and it convinced me even more that I enjoyed working. I could do most of the things she did and decided that, one day, I would be manager of a business. That ambition was good reason to do well in school, and I was fortunate to have good English and Math teachers. Lola Burke's goal in life seemed to be drilling the basics of English and grammar into her students, and I've always had an appreciation for her.

Living in what had been our rent house didn't affect me the way it did Mama and my older siblings. Losing that special home place was devastating for them, but this house, with its open fireplaces, had a special appeal for me. There were thirty acres of property with a barn, a smaller orchard and garden, and I enjoyed exploring them all.

Sylvia was only six years older than I, but the span seemed greater. She was Mama's ally and confidante, while I was grouped with the two younger ones and shielded from some realities. I was pretty naive and didn't understand that I was probably the most carefree member of my family. Even when Mama told me to help Sylvia with the housework, she didn't want help and preferred doing things alone. I did wash dishes and considered that drudgery, but I would have been glad to learn how to cook and bake.

Mama had been frail for months before Buford was born. Eight years old now, he was her seventh child and she'd had very little medical care. She seldom mentioned not feeling well, but Sylvia was running the household more and more. Graham was home and helping with the work, but some of his friends were working in Detroit and he planned to join them.

Returning from school one March afternoon, I was first off the bus. The other kids teased me about walking so fast they couldn't keep up, and I heard one say, "There she goes like she's shot from a cannon."

But I cared little for what they said. It was report card day and I was anxious for my mother to see mine. By the time they had sauntered across the bridge, I was halfway home. I took a shortcut through the orchard and followed the path to our kitchen door. The dog met me, wagging his tail, but I scolded him away and ran into the house calling, "Mama? Where are you?" But there was no answer and no one to be seen. Something was wrong. I had never come home to an empty house before.

I went out the front door and met Jewel coming from Aunt Lillie's. "We've been watching for you." she said, "and Aunt Lillie wants you to come straight to her house. Mama's real sick." I ran the short distance and saw Aunt Lillie had been crying. She told me Mama had begun hemorrhaging and Sylvia had called for her to come and help. A neighbor went to get David, and he and Sylvia took her to the doctor in Martin. She said, "David came back to tell me Dr. Stumbo sent Nancy to Beaver Valley Hospital, and she has to have surgery right away. He and Graham have gone to look for your father, for he has to sign permission to do the surgery."

My world turned upside down. Mama had been in the hospital before, but she'd never had surgery. Jewel and I went home, and soon my brothers were back. They hadn't found Papa but started looking again the next morning. They found him late in the day and took him directly to the hospital, but two days had been lost. They were frustrated and angry with him and anxious about the surgery.

Then it was over and everybody was relieved that she had come through it. Sylvia sent word she wasn't leaving the hospital till she could bring Mama home, and we'd just have to get along. I didn't know how to cook, but I put a few meals together and we tolerated them. We had canned foods to open and heat, and potatoes to bake or fry. I'd seen Mama make biscuits and decided to try it one morning, but mine were pitiful. We'd have to be starving to eat them. I gave one to the dog and he took it, like a bone, under a rose bush to chew on.

They did her surgery on a Friday but her condition was so serious we weren't allowed to go see her. Finally on Sunday she was a little better and wanted to see us. David took Jewel and me, and we were surprised to see her looking so pale with her head on that pillow. Sylvia said we could hug her if we'd be very gentle.

After five days there, with only a chair to rest in and a small bathroom for the barest necessities, Sylvia had been eating only what someone carried in for her. David insisted on taking her out to eat, and they left Jewel and me to visit. We stood, one on each side of her bed. Mama was weaker than I'd ever seen her. When she asked how we were doing at home, I told her about my biscuits. "What did you put in them?" she asked. When I told her, she said, "Sounds like you left out the baking powder. Use about two teaspoonfuls next time and they'll be all right." I said, "I'm not making any more till you show me. Graham made fun and said he was afraid he'd break a tooth. He went to the store and got some light bread, and we'll use that till you come home."

Sylvia wouldn't even stay away long enough to eat. She brought a hamburger and Pepsi to eat in the room and said, "David is waiting for you in the car, so you two had better run along." I kissed Mama good-bye and told her I'd be back soon. As I went bouncing down the stairs, I thought about my report card, and now I'd have to wait and tell her next time. Jewel was more reluctant to leave but knew she'd better cooperate or David wouldn't bring her again.

The next day, Monday, was the third day since Mama's surgery, and Aunt Zella came from Ashland to see her. She spent the afternoon at the hospital and then came to spend the night with us, bringing wonderful news. Mama was feeling much better. A few more good days and she should be coming home.

We were so happy that evening as we put supper together. I knew how to fix fried potatoes – we'd been having them every evening – so I started again. We had some ham and opened a can of beans. Aunt Zella made cornbread, and they were telling her how awful some of my cooking had been. We were in a mood to like anything after our good news, knowing our suppers would be better when Mama and Sylvia were home.

We let Aunt Zella make the bread, since I didn't know how, but she was "company" and we wouldn't let her wash dishes. Jewel and I did them as we bantered with her about her children, our cousins. She had twelve and there wasn't time to talk about them all, so we discussed the ones near our ages. Buford was in bed asleep before we finished the dishes, as we would have to get up early for school next morning.

We were all in bed and the last light turned out when there was a knock at the door. "Who would be coming at this hour?" I muttered as I climbed out of bed, straightened my gown and went to the door. It was Preacher Stratton. The hospital had called and asked him to come tell us Mama had died.

"No!" I screamed. "It can't be! They said she was better! No! No!"

My scream brought everybody out of bed, and Graham was pulling on clothes he'd just taken off. I couldn't accept it, couldn't stop repeating, "She can't be dead! No! No!" Graham came to me, still tugging on his shirt, put an arm around my shoulder and said, "You have to get a grip, Babe. Everybody needs us now, and I have to get to Sylvia for she's all alone." With that he was out the door – sweet, thoughtful Graham.

Jewel and Buford were crying, and Aunt Zella was trying to hold them both. Our dear old minister friend, who had walked the half mile to bring the news, still stood near the door as though trying to absorb some of our shock and sorrow. He could have had a ride with Graham back to his house but, as a minister of God, he seemed to sense his presence would mean some comfort to these broken hearts.

I ran to him crying, "Preacher Stratton, what will we do? What ever will we do?" He held me as I sobbed, and I could hear him repeating, "Bless your heart, child. Bless your little heart." Then I felt his own tears fall on my head.

Chapter 11
No Cinderella Here

After Preacher Stratton left that night, I just wandered through the house, feeling as if all hope were gone. Everything was still there – the furniture, curtains and pictures on the walls – and yet, if you tossed them all out, the house would have felt no more empty. My feelings then would cause me to forever equate grief with emptiness. I felt so totally lost without her. She hadn't been big on expressing her love, and yet it showed in her every act. There was no one to take her place. There had never been anyone else like her.

Friends and relatives came from everywhere. Our house seemed to swarm with people bringing food, flowers and gestures of kindness. Then the funeral was over and they were all gone, and the realization sank in that she was really gone. So many days could have been spelled d-a-z-e as we had no will to function. We ate because we had to.

No Cinderella Here

One of my haunting regrets was that I had done so little for her – I was always on the receiving end. For her last Mother's Day, I'd found a little serving bowl at the grocery store. It was white with a small yellow flower in the center, and it cost ten cents.

I knew nothing of gift wrapping or greeting cards and took it in a little brown paper bag. You would have thought I'd given her the moon, she seemed so pleased. Now I beat up on myself that I could have done so many little things for her. When I was younger, I sometimes picked a handful of violets and ran to her saying, "Look what I brought you!" and she put them in water as if they were roses. Why hadn't I done that more?

After the loss, we just felt our way along. Sylvia was totally exhausted from having stayed day and night at the hospital, and she pretty much fell apart. She was likely the most devastated of us all, but she'd been helping with housework so long that she'd learned how to manage. She soon took charge of the family and was most responsible for keeping us together and getting us grown up. She set rules and was pretty strict about them, and we did as she said without ever questioning. Graham joined his friends to work in Detroit, and he was her ally for support.

Papa gave us token attention and, in less than six months, he was married again. We couldn't understand that he would marry so soon. Did he think somebody different could bring our house alive again? We didn't even know who his new wife was but learned she was 39 and living with her parents and twin sister on Johns Creek. Her sister, also unmarried, was her only sibling, and they weren't accustomed to being around children. I never knew how they met.

No Cinderella Here

When he brought her to our house, it immediately became her house. We didn't know if she knew how to smile, for she had a forbidding look that we saw as an indication she was in charge. But the three youngest of us had learned to look to Sylvia for guidance. Just when we thought things could get no worse, Papa told Sylvia she should go live with Graham in Detroit because his new wife saw her as a rival in running the house. We were devastated that she'd leave us, not knowing it wasn't her idea. We just thought she and Graham would rather be together, and we wished we could be with them. That wasn't possible so we stayed busy with school and each other.

Jewel got permission to miss grade school one Thursday to go visit our high school, and we went together to catch the bus leaving Buford alone with the new wife. He was in third grade and getting ready to walk the short distance to school. It was Show and Tell day, a special time when students could bring a favorite toy to school. Buford was taking a little hammer Mama had given him but was ordered to, "Put that down!"

"It's mine," he countered, "and I'm taking it to school."

But she grabbed him by the throat and shook him saying, "You little shit! I'll show you!"

Buford ran to meet Jewel and me in the lane that evening, anxious to tell us what happened. We'd never been allowed to say that word, and Jewel, already afraid of her, began to cry. They thought she liked me better, but I was just bigger. She wasn't used to children and didn't really care for either of us. The incident wouldn't have happened had we all been there, but we had to be apart some. I was bewildered but knew we'd have to look out for ourselves – and for each other. This was my little brother, but more than that, he was Mama's baby, and I wasn't going to let anyone mistreat him.

Supper time was no longer the cordial banter we'd known in earlier days, but that evening was unusually quiet. Each was absorbed in his or her own thoughts, and I was thinking the three of us were a pretty vulnerable bunch. I didn't know the word, but I knew its meaning.

The others finished eating first and left Jewel and me at the table. Papa and his wife had gone into the next room and we heard her say, "You'll have to make the girls wash the dishes. I've put out a washing today and I'm tired." Just like a robot, he walked in and said. "You girls will have to wash the dishes. She's put out a washing today, and she's tired." So this is the way it's going to be, I was thinking – or at least the way they intend it to be. Washing the dishes was no big deal, but being ordered this way was. I just looked at him and said, "Okay."

When he left the room, I turned to Jewel and asked, "Do you want to wash the dishes or go to the store? We're going to make a cake and we need two eggs." (We could have bought one egg at our store if we wished.) She said, "I'll go to the store," and Buford agreed he'd go with her. Our elders had gone to bed before I had the dishes done, as I knew they would. We weren't very good at baking, but we had our cake. When we went to bed, we left bowls with batter mix, pans stuck with dried cake and beaters with dried icing. We left plates and forks and glasses, but we had washed the supper dishes.

My differences weren't so much with her anyway. Had we met under different circumstances, we likely would have been friendly, but being thrown together this way was a real misfit. We weren't her charges, and Papa seemed to feel no responsibility for us. Buford didn't even tell him about the shaking episode. As young as he was, he realized there was no point.

    We hadn't planned to bake the cake or wreck the kitchen so it wasn't so much an action as a reaction. Up to this time I'd been pretty passive about whatever Papa did or didn't do, but a new fire flamed in me and every neglect he'd ever imposed on any of the family came into focus. I'd read fairy tales and knew I was no kin to Cinderella, and I already decided there had to be a father somewhere who overlooked his children. There would be no glass slipper for me, for I refused to be the stereotypical stepchild, even if it cost me everything – and it almost did. The next day was Friday and we had a ball game that night. Fellow cheerleader, Virginia Allen, invited me to spend the night, and Jewel was glad to accept an invitation from one of her friends since I'd be away. I learned after the fact what happened next. The new wife decided she was going back home to Johns Creek, but she didn't just go.

    Aunt Lillie and Uncle Tom lived just across the road and saw him back the car as close to the front steps as he could and wait, with the car running, while she carried load after load to fill the trunk and back seat. She took all her clothes and most of his. A neighbor met them leaving and threw up his hand; then he glanced at the house and saw smoke coming from it and called to Uncle Tom. "That house is on fire!"

    This dear uncle was paralyzed and could do nothing, but he asked the neighbor to run out to the school and ask the teachers to send some of the biggest boys. That wouldn't be

No Cinderella Here

allowed today, but times were different and Mr. Franklin came with them to find Aunt Lillie and a few neighbors organizing a bucket brigade from the little stream called Rice Branch.

The doors had been left unlocked, so Mr. Franklin stepped carefully inside to see where the fire originated, but he found no flames – just smoke coming from under a closet door near the kitchen. A big eighth grader, Wade, found an axe in the smokehouse and climbed up to chop a hole in the roof. Smoke and flames shot out and they knew where to throw the water that the boys kept providing. Soon the fire was extinguished, and our only loss was a hole in the roof and the contents of the food closet, our main supply of food for the winter – food that had taken long days and hours to grow and preserve.

Mr. Franklin wanted to be sure the fire was all out, so he went to the closet where he first saw the smoke. What he found among the broken glass was soaked paper, rags, boxes and even two soppy lumps of coal, so he told Uncle Tom the fire had been set. The wife hadn't just struck a match; she had shoveled hot coals from the coal stove to be sure it burned. Whether or not Papa knew what she was doing, he certainly knew what she'd done – everybody knew.

Aunt Lillie talked some of the boys into coming back Saturday, after the mess had cooled, to clean out the closet. They dug a big hole in the lower end of the garden and used a wheelbarrow and shovel to bury the spilled food and broken glass. We should have put up a marker to read: Beans, Corn, Apples, Tomatoes, Tomato juice, Kraut, Pickles, Jams, Jellies, Applesauce... anything we'd grown that could be preserved. Even with the loss, it was fortunate the fire began there, for every time a jar broke some juice or wet food served to retard the fire until help came.

One thing I've learned about angels is that they keep a low profile. In fact, they're seldom recognized at all. They like giving people opportunities to help, and I can imagine those happy schoolboys telling their families what they'd done. At no time in my life were these divine beings ever more present than in saving that house for us. It held every personal thing we owned – our beds, our clothing, our shelter against the world. We couldn't even bemoan the loss of food with so much left, and a strange thing was that, any time we felt hungry, there was always something good to eat. Somehow the cupboard was never bare.

When Sylvia and Graham learned we'd been abandoned, he brought her home and all seemed right with our world. We felt secure with her, and when we learned she'd been forced to leave, we felt betrayed all over again.

Graham went back to his job and continued to send money for us as he always did when it was needed. At the ages of eighteen and twenty, they were now head of the family, and we all worked together for whatever needs and wishes we had. We knew we'd always grieve for the mother we'd lost so soon, but we could sense her presence with us and felt she was pleased with the way we cared for each other.

Chapter 12
High School Days

It was really good to get settled into school, and it didn't take long to understand this was a whole new world. The very first day in Mr. Steele's History class was when Walter Hall whacked me in the head with a paper wad. When class ended, he came to offer an apology, and I told him it was okay. It was more than okay – it was wonderful! I thought he was the cutest boy I'd ever seen but that he was picking on me because I was the new kid in class.

Whatever I thought, he was determined to know me better, and soon I was hearing whispers that "Aileen took Walter from Ella." I knew nothing of another girlfriend, but it was apparent he had lost all interest there.

When I lost my mother four months later, I was so heartbroken that I couldn't have been very good company to anyone. But Walter took notice of my sadness and seemed to

really care. His attention and the classes I had to prepare for helped me get through that year.

I was flattered to think he liked me, for he was one of the most popular boys in school. He was on the basketball team and had a great personality, but we could only see each other at school for I lived on Prater Creek, eight miles away.

As the school year was ending, I told him I was enrolling in summer school, and he decided he would too. Mrs. Howard was his English teacher and she gave a test the first day to see what the students already knew about the subject. "That way," she said, "I'll know what to cover."

Walter said, "A teacher who gives a test the first day is too tough for me," and he dropped out. He didn't need the credits anyway, but he lived within walking distance of school and made it a point to be there to share a Coke at the Bobcat Inn. School had become more interesting than I expected. Each classmate was unique and getting to know them was a never-ending interest. Young as we were, our experiences together were real, and lasting bonds were forged. No wonder so many friendships endure long after school days are over.

Principal D. W. Howard was one of the most agreeable personalities I ever knew. When we were a little slow to settle down for open assembly he announced, "Now children, we just want to live and let live." He wasn't big on scolding and his methods were effective.

One of his favorite stories was about his earlier teaching days when he caught then-first-grader Palmer Crum skipping school and playing out by the gym. Seeing the teacher approach, Palmer said, "Mr. Howa'd, there's a mama fwog under this fwoor, and I fink she's got witt ones."

He said, "Well, Palmer, those little ones will still be there when school is out, but right now you need to get into class to learn how to read and write." He told that story long after Palmer grew up to be a star baseball player and one of the first inductees into the town's Hall of Fame.

Mr. Howard had a sense of humor that was contagious and he could laugh at himself when the joke was on him. Mrs. Howard, on the other hand, was a stickler for proper decorum. Once she got a bit carried away in giving a classroom lecture on respect. She'd overheard a student call a teacher by his first name and was appalled.

She said, "If you'll notice, Mr. Howard and I don't use our first names here at school. When we''re home, we're Delmon and Myrtle, but here at school, we're Mr. and Mrs. Howard. Neither of us would ever use first names because we want to set the right example for you students."

Just then the door flew open and her husband rushed in. "Myrtle, do you know where my keys are? I've looked everywhere and can't find them!" The whole class erupted into laughter, and there went the lesson on respect.

Carlos Hale was a delightful personality who taught Literature and Music, directed the glee club and led the high school band that played for ball games and other sports events. I loved the band music and being in her class, and her caring manner made her a favorite of many of us.

I didn't mind the writing assignments or memorizing poetry but, in our junior year, we were required to make a five minute speech before the student body. I dreaded it like nothing else in school. When the day came, I was petrified. Somehow I got through it, but I determined I would never make a public speech again in all my life.

High School Days

During my sophomore year, I got a job working the lunch hour at the Liberty Bell Café where many of the students ate. It was owned by Jim and Angelyn George who paid me 25 cents an hour. I always loved working, and any pay was great. You could eat lunch for a quarter, and a Pepsi was a nickel.

The Georges had a service station along with the café, and one day Jim said, "If you have any extra time, I need some help with the bookkeeping and running this place."  I was delighted by that and could make time. He raised my pay to 35 cents, and soon I was working Saturdays and any time I wasn't in school. I pumped gas, made sandwiches and kept records. Between classes and working at the Liberty Bell, I was glad for every opportunity to see Walter. One Saturday, after I'd worked half a day, he got his dad's car and came to take me for a drive. My good friend Anna Layne was there, and Bernard Clark just happened to stop by. We asked them to join us and, against better judgment, we all four piled into the front seat.

We were going toward Prestonsburg and, just as we rounded a curve near the Davidson Cemetery, we met a state

police. He gave us a good look and slowed down, and we knew he'd be coming back; but he was in the curve and had to turn around. Walter said, "Quick, Bernard! Climb into the back!"

Cars didn't have seat belts then and, when the policeman pulled us over, Bernard was sitting on the edge of the back seat with his face up near ours as though he'd been there all the time. The officer checked Walter's driver's license and, seeing nothing amiss, said, "You kids have fun, but be careful." It just added excitement to our day to think we got away with something, and that's about as wild as we got.

From time to time, Walter brought me little presents – a necklace or some piece of jewelry – and I wondered how he did it since he seldom had money for a movie or anything that cost admission.

We had little spats now and then and, on one such occasion, I gave his gifts back. A few days later, the cutest little girl came up to me and said, "I'm Betty, Walter's sister, and Mother sure was glad to get her jewelry back. She thought it was gone forever."

So that's how he was able to afford my gifts! I thought it was funny, and when the spat was over, I got to know his family better.

There was a lot of hype about the Junior/Senior prom as we had almost no formal activities. I'd never been very clothes conscious, but I just had to have a formal dress. Sylvia and Graham saw that I got one. She went to town and came back with a pretty yellow one, just my size. I'd never seen myself in anything so elegant.

I could expect Walter to bring me home after the prom, but his father wouldn't be home with the car in time for him to

pick me up, so I had to get there some other way. My friend Gladys lived by the bridge and offered me a ride, but she couldn't drive the unpaved road to pick me up. I didn't mind walking, but I probably puzzled the neighbors, going down that dusty road in my long dress and sandals.

Walter had begun smoking cigarettes even then, but there was no alcohol, and we'd never heard of the drugs some people used in later years. It was exciting for us all to see each other dressed up, and I was especially pleased to have a sweetheart telling me how pretty he thought I looked.

I truly enjoyed my role as cheerleader for the Bobcats. Our uniforms were short pleated skirts and sweaters in the blue and white school colors, and we wore white socks and saddle oxfords. We didn't have majorettes for the band, so our presence was expected throughout the games. We weren't all acrobats, but Virginia Allen could turn handsprings and cartwheels up and down the gym floor, and that fascinated me. I needed time and room to do a somersault, but Jenny made up for any shortcomings the rest of us had. We had pep rallies before games and did all we could to nurture a team spirit.

Sometimes I stayed overnight with my friend Anna on ball game nights, and we could walk to the gym. But going from home meant walking the mile to catch the school bus and returning after dark. There were usually four or five of us to walk together and we didn't mind.

But one night, returning from a game at Garrett, I started looking for my buddies on the bus. I learned one was staying over with a friend, and another was sick. I don't know about the others, but neither was on the bus. That meant I had to walk home alone.

We didn't have cell phones and there was no way to contact someone to meet me. Had I known in time, I could have gone home with Anna, but this was totally unexpected.

The moon was pretty bright, it was around 10:30, and I was hurrying along trying to convince myself I wasn't afraid. Then I thought about having to pass the Spears' house, and everybody knew they had a vicious dog. They had a sturdy fence with a gate that latched and kept him confined in the yard, but the boys I walked with always carried a stick to feel safer.

When I rounded the curve in sight of the house, I could see in the moonlight the gate was hanging open. Then as I got closer, I saw the dog. He didn't run or bark; he was creeping at me with a low growl that sounded eerie. I did know not to run, and I'd always heard to never let a dog know you were afraid as that only made them more vicious, but you can't conceal fright.

I couldn't have run anyway for he was coming at me with bared teeth, and I simply froze. I wanted to scream, hoping the family would hear me, but my throat seemed paralyzed and I couldn't make a sound.

He was within two feet of me and snarling at my bare legs when suddenly he yelped and darted back through the open gate. I didn't have a clue about what happened. He was just gone and I wasn't injured, but I was an emotional wreck and cried the rest of the way home.

Some days later, I went to the Saturday Bible class Fred and Dorthea McGinnis taught at the old schoolhouse. Their lesson was about the angels charged with our keeping, though we don't always see them. They told about Balaam who was

riding his donkey and, though he beat it, he couldn't make it go where he directed. That's because, "...the donkey saw the Angel of the Lord standing in the way with his sword drawn in His hand, and the donkey turned aside out of the way and went into the field." (Numbers 22:23)

That story is the only explanation I ever had about my protection that night. I didn't see the Angel walking with me – but I saw evidence that He was there.

Chapter 13
The Courtship

Our courtship actually began the day we first saw each other. The paper wad incident gave way to other flirtations and an eager awareness of each other's presence.

I was very shy while Walter was outgoing, popular and good looking. His attention was exciting and it boosted my self-confidence. He played guard on the basketball team and that helped me get up the courage to try out for cheerleader. I was thrilled to be chosen by the student body and to know I'd get to be part of the action. Even more than that, we'd have opportunities to see each other more often.

In the middle of our sophomore year, I was standing on the sideline with the other cheerleaders. It was halftime intermission in a game with the McDowell Dare Devils when Walter walked over and said with a bit of urgency, "Come with me. Coach wants something from his car."

Teacher Aaron Akers was monitoring the door and stopped us. "You know you're not allowed to leave the gym unless you're going home."

The Courtship

"But Mr. Akers," Walter protested, "we're just going to get something. We're coming right back."

He was still reluctant, but said, "Make it quick and I'll wait right here."

Walter led the way to a car parked over by a bus and urged me to hurry. When I caught up, he leaned against the car door and, as though he thought me fragile enough to break, put a hand on my left shoulder and kissed me very softly.

He tilted his head back and said, "I've wanted to do that since the first day I saw you." Then he kissed me again, a little more firmly this time, grabbed my hand and said, "Let's go." As we hurried back into the gym, I asked, "What did you come after, anyway?" He laughed as he answered, "That was it!"

As we ran past Mr. Akers, he had a quizzical look as if he expected Walter to be carrying something; but just then the whistle blew signaling the start of the second half. I had trouble concentrating on the rest of the game for thinking he actually wanted to kiss me. When the game was over, he escorted me to the bus and said, "I'll see you tomorrow."

Even with war news blaring every day and young men leaving for service, we were normal teenagers who, at times, had disagreements and tried to act disinterested in one another. During one such time, I had just sat down in Civics class and our teacher, Mrs. Coy, said, "Get your books out. You'll need them open today." Emmit Conn, who sat across the aisle to my left, said, "I don't have a book, Aileen. Can I share yours?"

The Courtship

"Sure," I answered, and he scooted his seat over beside me. His desk had an arm on the left side, and the right side was against mine which made him totally hemmed in. Walter came into the room a few minutes late and, seeing Emmit that close to me, walked over and socked him.

Mrs. Coy cried out in a high pitched voice, "Boys! Boys!" and sent them both to the principal's office. Emmit was totally innocent and, telling about it later added, "I wasn't even interested in her. I just didn't have a book."

Walter had tried to be so cool and had made a point of looking the other way when he saw me, but this reaction let me know how he really felt. I was sorry about Emmit, but I was glad too, for I very much wanted him to care. After making up, our feelings for each other were even more intense.

One of our favorite recreations was dancing at Dick Layne's Dance Hall. Dick and his wife, Delsie, ran a restaurant where we could eat sandwiches, have a Coke or Pepsi and dance to music on the juke box. Dick was a former state police who knew how to maintain order but there wasn't much policing required for our group. We used up our energy dancing to the music of Glenn Miller, Benny Goodman, Tommy Dorsey, Duke Ellington, Woody Herman and others. Some of our favorite tunes were *In The Mood, String of Pearls,* and *Tuxedo Junction* by Glen Miller. I especially loved Tommy Dorsey's *Boogie Woogie* and *Song of India,* but we liked most of the music of our day.

Walter was a better dancer than I, but it didn't matter a lot. I could do pretty well and it was fun. We enjoyed just being in a classroom together, but dancing was a means of touching. And in a slow dance, he could hold me close. That was really nice. Some of the kids were such good dancers that when they took the floor to do the jitterbug the rest of us just sat back and watched. It was fun to be with the group we'd become a part of, and Dick and Delsie were good to all of us.

When school went out in June, I had a chance to go to Detroit and visit David and his family. Graham also worked there now and was dating a girl named Delilah. She was 21, all grown-up and, I thought, very sophisticated. Probably because I was Graham's sister, she took an interest in me and set out to make my visit a good one. She took me to the Fox Theater to see a live performance by big band leader Les Brown and his Band of Renown. We got along great and she asked if I'd like to get a job for a few weeks before school started again. She had room for me at her apartment, and that sounded exciting.

She took me to Greenfield's Restaurant where she worked and introduced me to the manager who said I could work as a waitress even though I was only sixteen. Pay was much better than at the Liberty Bell. I didn't know the first thing about waiting tables and dealing with so many people on that scale. Also, customers teased me about my Kentucky accent. But the other employees, especially Delilah, helped me get better at the job, and just when I was beginning to adapt, it was time to come home for school again.

Walter was glad to see me back, and he borrowed a truck to haul a canoe for us to launch in the Big Sandy

The Courtship

River. We had great fun for a while, but I didn't know much about canoes and I stepped to one side and flipped us right into the river. We had on regular clothes and got sopping wet, shoes and all. We just kept laughing and it added to the excitement of our day. Even getting dunked was fun if we could be together.

Summer was ending, the war was escalating and our whole world was changing. We were very young, but we knew we were in love. I don't remember that he actually proposed. He just began saying, "When we get married..."

We had no idea when that could ever be. We needed more education, the war had to end, and it would be a long time before we could support ourselves. But we knew that, however long it took, we were meant for each other.

Chapter 14
The Last Straw

The days were flying by and, when school began in August, Walter and I were seniors – part of the class of 1944. We tried to maintain that special mood seniors are supposed to enjoy, but there was always the war to think of. Anything that wasn't crucial to the war effort would be foregone, and that meant we had no school annual for our last two years. Even more crucial was the fact that Walter was 17 and could expect to be drafted after graduation.

He wanted to be a Marine and knew that, if he waited to be drafted, he might not be able to choose his branch of service. He talked of volunteering and it made me cringe, but every loyal American was caught up in the conflict. There were groups organized to gather scrap metal, some made bandages and other supplies for the wounded, and many people were donating blood – anything at all to win this war.

Then one morning he came to school and announced, "I've volunteered. I'm a brand new member of the U. S. Marine Corps!" He had given his age as eighteen, though it wasn't quite that, and he'd be leaving soon for training at Parris Island, South Carolina. He had enough credits to graduate but it wouldn't have mattered if he didn't.

My world was shattered, but I promised, "I'll write every day." And he kept mentioning, "When I get back and we can get married…" And then he was gone.

School took on a new meaning after he left. Nothing was as much fun any more, but the basketball season wasn't over. He was replaced at the guard position, and the cheerleading continued, but now I made a point of writing a letter every day.

After a few weeks at Parris Island, he was transferred to Camp Le Jeune, North Carolina, for further training and his parents, Richard and Era, were allowed to visit him. He told them not to come without me and they were very gracious to take me along. The visit was just for a weekend and it flew by. We could see he was toughening up. Also, they had cut his hair very short and he looked different.

Soon he was shipped out for overseas duty and we had no idea when we'd see him again. The battles were being waged in many locations, but he could never tell us where he was. His mail to us was censored, and sometimes portions of his letters were cut out if he gave any indication of where he was. Newspapers were treasured and radios blared everywhere.

The Last Straw

I was already writing letters to Graham who was serving aboard ship in some undisclosed location. He had terrible bouts of seasickness that made him miserable. He was trained as a communications specialist and spent much of his time on a sub chaser, but we never knew where.

While working in Detroit, Graham had sent money to Sylvia for our support. His pay as a sailor was less, but he made an allotment to her. If she could save any for him, that would be good; but if she didn't, that was okay too.

Papa came by the house once in a while in some semblance of checking on us. We never expected him and didn't miss him, but he was still Papa and we answered his questions. He knew we were resourceful and looked out for each other, and we always told him we were doing all right.

One day he came by when I really needed something. I thought maybe he didn't understand the struggles we were dealing with, and I told him, "In case you don't know, it's a little hard going to school without enough money for lunch, clothes and books. I've decided I'm going to quit school." I'd always made good grades and I knew teachers had told him what a good student I was. I thought my announcement was pretty drastic and I fully expected him to say something like, "Oh no, we'll just have to find you some help." Instead he said, "Do whatever you want to do."

It was the last straw, and I just stared at him thinking, "You don't really care!" As much as I'd seen, I was still caught off guard. Somehow I'd felt circumstances would change at the right time and there would be a way to attend college, but any hope I had died that day – and I gave up on him that day. I knew I'd never quit school, but I'd also never ask him for anything again.

The Last Straw

Giving up was pretty drastic. I thought of college as being some sort of mill that, once you went through it, you were capable of doing whatever you wished, so giving up meant more than feeling some disappointment. It meant the end of a dream.

Papa didn't come back for a while and one of our neighbors told us he had a new baby girl. Sylvia and I went to

the hospital to see her. She was a pretty little thing, and the mother actually smiled as we talked about her. They named the baby Georgean, and she would be two years old before we saw her again.

Even with the war, it was important to our class that we graduate, and we had to continue our studies and tests. Our sweethearts and friends were still a central part of our lives – many were just long distance now.

My sister Jewel was a freshman during my senior year, and she was popular from the start. She had blond hair, pretty blue eyes and an 18-inch waist. She also had a beautiful voice that enhanced the music program at school. We didn't get to cheerlead together as she was elected the year after I graduated.

Nobody had told me scholarships were available to outstanding students so I had only tried to make good grades and graduate. I wasn't supposed to be on the program for graduation, but my Literature teacher had one more assignment. I was to deliver the class prophecy, projecting what each class member would be doing twenty years down the road.

Principal D. W. Howard was an amiable and well liked teacher and a pleasant influence on so many of us. W. D. Steele was a History teacher who knew how to maintain discipline and still be popular with the student body. They both sat on the stage for our program.

I created a likely role for each student and made them doctors, lawyers, merchants, chiefs. Some had big families, and some were lone rangers, but all were successful.

One of the prophecies was about Wendell Stratton. I projected that he would marry his high school sweetheart, Lora Jean Clark, and live on a farm at Ivel with twin boys, one named named D. W. and the other W. D. As I read my prophecy, the two teachers just looked at each other, but the audience almost fell out of their seats.

I was seventeen, and I thought my dream of continuing my education had been crushed. I had no idea how many avenues I would find for learning – intelligent friends, books, training institutes, writers' workshops, everyday living. You'd almost have to close your eyes and ears to not absorb what you needed.

Chapter 15
Life in the City

*J*was seventeen when I graduated from high school and could hardly wait to get back to Detroit. Having worked those few weeks at Greenfield's last summer, I was anxious to earn my way at last. Sylvia wanted only to be at home, and it would be just her, Jewel and Buford now. But we would write each other often.

She helped me find some luggage and get ready, and I rode the C & O passenger train to Ashland. There I boarded the Sportsman for travel on to Detroit. Its schedule ran at night, and it was so crowded you couldn't even nap on the way. In fact, if you didn't stay alert, your head might fall on some stranger's shoulder.

I had kept in touch with Delilah and knew she would still help me, but nothing had come of her dating Graham. He was now in the Navy, and she had married somebody else. She said her younger sister, Alice Marie, had graduated from high school and wanted to come there to work. I hadn't met Alice yet, but we could live together.

Estill and Opal would soon be moving to Oakland, California, and I lived with them for a short while, until we'd earned enough for rent. Then, with Delilah's help, Alice and I got a small furnished apartment on Davenport Street.

We didn't live there long, for Delilah's marriage hadn't worked out, and we got a bigger place on Brainard Street where she could live with us. It wasn't hard to move; we just had our clothing and enough sheets and towels for light housekeeping.

Greenfield's had hired us on the spot. They needed healthy girls willing to work and serve their many customers. We all dressed alike in the sparkling white uniforms they provided and were taught the proper etiquette for setting tables. It was a popular eating place, and sometimes customers stood in long lines just to get in. They chose their own food, but we arranged it on the table and saw they had water and the needed silverware. If they wanted anything more, we would get it and help make their meal enjoyable.

The time I spent working there was the college education I didn't have. The things I learned weren't from books, but rather in living. The clientele came from all walks of life and one thing they all had in common was a taste for delicious food.

The restaurant was owned by Fred Simonsen, and once in a while he and his wife came in to eat and see how things were going. The daytime manager was C.L. Henry, and I thought he was dignity personified. He wore immaculate suits and was an ideal manager who ran a pretty efficient ship.

Olie Barry was the evening manager, very likeable and in control, but a little more laid back.

We had an employees' dining room and separate lounges for men and women where we each had a locker for our personal belongings. We wore our own clothing to work and changed into fresh uniforms each day. There was always a new supply in each of our sizes. When we clocked out, we dropped our soiled uniform in a laundry chute.

Some of the girls smoked in the women's lounge and, wanting to be like them, I gave it a try. I fairly choked and have always been glad I didn't like it.

Both customers and fellow employees were merciless in teasing me about my accent. They laughed at me for saying "you all," but I thought it was better than their expression of "youse guys." I never lost my accent, but I did learn to drop some expressions strange to them.

Life in the City

The restaurant was open 20 hours a day and closed from 2:00 to 6:00 a.m. for cleaning. I worked days, 9:00 to 5:00 for a time, but preferred evenings, from 3:00 to 11:00. The mood of the daytime customers was more serious and their tips smaller, while the evening crowd was more relaxed and more generous. We got the show crowd and sometimes the performers too.

Several people were regular customers and we got to know them pretty well. Two of these were Bill and Mary who were there one evening when I helped a distinguished looking gentleman and his party get seated and ready to eat. When I walked away, Mary called to me, "Aileen, do you know who you just waited on?" Of course I didn't. She said, "That's Fred Vinson, Chief Justice of the Supreme Court." He was from Louisa, Kentucky, but I hadn't known who he was.

One customer I did recognize was Max Schmeling, the famous boxer. And there were many others – Sonja Henie, the skating star, the Kramer Midgets and Rita Moreno, who was a young and aspiring actress.

One night when the circus was in town, there was an armless girl who ate with her feet. She wore long pants, banded at the ankle, but she was agile and did great with her meal. In cases like that, the manager very discreetly reminded us not to stare, but it was hard to keep from it.

There was another group I'd never heard of, dressed as men but with such feminine traits it was puzzling. I learned they were gays, but that wasn't the term people used then.

Our apartment was only a few blocks from Greenfield's on Woodward Avenue, so we often walked to work. We tried walking home a few times, but realized it wasn't safe at night. We had a few real scares with men trying to pick us up and we started taking a cab. Even then we tried to travel together. There wasn't a problem involving drugs but there were many dangers, and I couldn't be careful enough in my own strength and wisdom to always protect myself. In some cases, I know, my guardian angel was put on overtime.

Back at the apartment, I always took time to write a few letters – to Graham, Sylvia, and always to Walter. Sometimes when he wrote to me, he said, "Still no mail today. I haven't heard from you for twelve days." He thought I wasn't writing, but when mail caught up with him there would be fourteen letters. I wrote to him every day while he was away.

Of course I reported any news of home which included the shock of Americans that President Franklin D. Roosevelt had died on April 12, 1945, and Vice President Harry Truman succeeded him. I was at work that day and saw customers visibly shaken by the news.

During the latter part of 1945, a letter came from Walter with a money order. He wrote, "I've wanted so much to put a ring on your finger, but I'm so far away. I want you to have some symbol of our engagement, so please go choose yourself a ring for me and, every time you look at it, know how much I love you."

I went that very afternoon to a jeweler downtown and chose a beautiful diamond ring. It wasn't huge, but it had sparkle and it fit my finger perfectly. I was elated and had to describe it to him in all the ways I could.

On our days off from work, we sometimes took the river boat cruise to Bob-Lo Island across the Detroit River from Windsor, Canada. Alice and I liked to have lunch at one of the hotdog stands or deli shops on Belle Isle. We rented bicycles and rode all around the island.

At other times, we went to the city park on Cass Avenue just to see the trees, grass and children playing. It was the closest thing we had to Kentucky.

We went to theaters to see shows or live performances by Frank Sinatra, band leaders Harry James, Sammy Kay and others. You were invited to *Swing and Sway with Sammy Kay*.

One of the popular songs of the day was *Sentimental Journey* by Harry James, and it always made me cry. I felt homesick for people and places I had loved and lost. I think it just aroused a sentiment to cry – for my mother, for Graham and for Walter. I could always cry for my mother, but I missed them all.

Another Beverly sister, Vivian, dated a pilot named Charlie. They came to the apartment just to check on us one day and Alice said, "Charlie, I'd really like to take a plane ride." I added, "Me too! I've never been up in a plane."

He said, "Well, if you can come out to the airport Tuesday morning at ten, I'll take you."

It was a small plane called a Piper Cub, and he took us up one at a time. Alice went first and said it was great, and then it was my time. When he reached the right altitude, he began tilting the plane to show me the landmarks below.

We talked about the view and he pointed out, "That's Ford Motor Company off to your left, there's the water tower, and that's Grosse Point and . . ." He glanced at me and said, "Aileen, you're green!" I could only nod my head.

He wore a pilot's cap with a strap under the chin, but he took it off and tossed it to me saying. "There, just in case." It was just barely in time, for I threw up in it and he had to discard it when we landed.

Life in the City

While we lived there, the city had blackouts fairly often. When the sirens sounded, everyone knew to get lights out and the city became really dark. Even traffic stopped. You never knew if it was a practice or a real warning of attack, for Detroit was a major weapons producing center. I was always fortunate to be inside during the alert, but nothing moved until the all clear sounded.

Another danger arose when race riots broke out. The city was in turmoil for days as violence erupted all over town and became national news. Cars were overturned and burned in the streets, and fights broke out wherever people clashed. We didn't have TV then, but radios blared the news and newspapers flashed the headlines. It was the beginning of the end of segregation.

At one time, I began getting a sore throat and missed work for a day or two. A doctor said my adenoids needed to come out and I was scheduled for surgery. Sylvia wanted to come to be with me but said she wouldn't be able to leave Jewel and Buford.

I didn't think Mr. Henry knew anything about me except that I liked working but, a couple of days before I went to the hospital, he called me aside to say, "I hear you're having some surgery."

"Yes," I said.

"Do you have any family here?"

"No, but I have friends."

Then he surprised me. "Is there anything at all you need?"

My eyes misted but I couldn't say, "No one ever asked me that before." I had the greatest respect for him and was touched by it.

Then I laughed at myself and said, "No, but thanks so much, and I'm sure I'll do fine."

When they took me to surgery at Ford Hospital, I'd been completely at ease until they put on the mask to give me ether. After a few seconds, I decided I didn't know any of those people and I wasn't going to breathe that stuff. I'd not go to sleep. Suddenly the mask clamped down on my face and started slinging me around the room, and that's the way I went to sleep.

When I awoke, the first person I saw was Sylvia. She had ridden the train all night to come and be with me, thinking she just had to come. I was really miserable, and she was a welcome sight.

When I returned to work I was asked a little more often to relieve a cashier for lunch break. There were always two, one to add the items on a tray and ring up the check, and the other to collect the money and make change. They saw I could do either task well and offered me the job full time. I would have a raise and wouldn't be wearing a uniform or have to walk so much.

But I was eighteen, and what did I care for walking? I loved being all over the place, bantering with the customers and matching notes with the other girls, especially Eva and Flo, two sisters from Clintwood. Virginia. Mr. Henry thought I'd be pleased but understood I'd rather be "on the floor."

Alice and I were close in age and became lifelong friends, but it was Delilah I had bonded with and relied on for almost everything. If Sylvia was responsible for getting me grown up, it was she who helped me make the transition to adulthood.

Life in the City

My knowledge of cosmetics was mostly a bar of Ivory soap and a tube of Colgate toothpaste, but she taught me to use lotions and powder, how to shave my legs and wear nylon hose, how to shape my eyebrows and choose lipstick to match my coloring.

She took me to Hudson's downtown store for my first few clothing purchases and taught me to travel around by streetcar. If she first liked me for my brother, she now pretty much adopted me for myself.

Delilah worked an earlier shift than Alice or me. She helped train new employees and liked to be able to go on dates in the evening. Sometimes when I got in from work, she would already be asleep. The door would wake her and she'd say, "Is that you, Elleen?" She always pronounced my name differently.

"Are you asleep already?" I asked. "I need a shampoo and hoped you would help me." She just muttered, "Oh, you kid!" Then after a bit, she said, "Go ahead and wash your hair and I'll help you with the curlers."

We'd usually have something to share about our day, and then wind up making a cup of hot chocolate before turning in.

And there was the night I got a toothache and couldn't sleep. We tried different ways to stop the pain, and then she just sat with me. When business hours began in the morning, she called and arranged for a dentist to see me. I took a cab to and from his office.

When I returned, she asked, "Did he fix it?"

"No," I said, "he pulled it." Then I boo-hooed.

She was bewildered, "Well, does it still hurt?"

"No, but I lost a tooth."

She burst out laughing and I was appalled; but she hadn't expected me to cry. When she saw how devastated I was, she became a little more compassionate – but not much.

As much as anyone I've ever known, Delilah had class. I don't know how she'd become so proficient in making her way, but she exemplified good manners and responsibility.

I'd like to think just a little of that rubbed off on me.

Chapter 16
Wedding Bells

The atomic bomb, the most destructive device of all time, was perfected in the spring of 1945. On August 6, it was used to kill more than 80,000 people in Hiroshima and almost as many again three days later in Nagasaki. At the time, we didn't think so much about how agonizing the decision to use those bombs must have been for President Truman and Prime Minister Churchill. We were just acutely aware that our nation was at war and thousands of our troops were being killed.

Germany had already signed terms of surrender in May, and on August 15, six days after the bombing of Nagasaki, Japan announced its surrender to the Allied Forces. The war would not officially end until the ceremony aboard the USS Missouri on September 2, but the celebration didn't wait.

Alice and I slept late on that August day after Japan surrendered. Rushing around to get ready for work, we didn't

Wedding Bells

turn the radio on. We didn't understand, as we hurried down Woodward Avenue to our jobs, why so many car horns were blowing and people waving from their windows. When we walked into the restaurant, the whole atmosphere was different. Customers were animated and talking to each other from table to table, something very rare to see.

We stopped by the cashier's desk to ask what was going on, and Peggy squealed, "Japan surrendered! Didn't you hear?" I felt like yelling, "Whoopee!" right there, for I knew the end of the war was in sight.

By November, Graham was safely home from the Navy, but Walter would not be released for several more months. The fact that both survived the war seemed like a miracle to me. My heart ached for families who had lost sons and daughters, and I felt so grateful and blessed that Walter would be coming home. It wasn't until much later that I learned he had been in the invasion of Okinawa where almost 50,000 Marines lost their lives in one campaign.

I celebrated my nineteenth birthday in December and a final Christmas with my friends in Detroit. At work, I bubbled over with excitement about my guy coming home and our plans to get married. As that long awaited day approached, I walked into the employees' dining room and there on the bulletin board in big bold letters, I saw, For Sale: One Pair of Shoes – Aileen is Going Home!

It was like a farewell party in our dining room that day. One of my co-workers presented me with a set of figurines she said depicted the way Walter and I would look when I met him at the airport.

Walter received his discharge at Great Lakes, Illinois on May 14, 1946. A celebration had been planned for returning

Wedding Bells

Marines, but he didn't wait for it. He took the first flight he could get over to Detroit and I was there to meet him, looking much like the wide-eyed figurine. Excited as I was, I was aware of the gawking eyes watching us, but the skinny boy who once stole a kiss in the school parking lot was all grown up now and didn't care if the whole world was watching. We laughed, and I cried, and I thought he would never let me go. All those months of separation, all those letters written, all those times of not knowing if it would ever happen, and now he was here. It was a dream come true!

Walter had always been confident, but he had matured. And the shy little girl from Prater Creek, while making her way in the city, had done some growing up too. We were still young but we were ready to begin our new life together.

He bought a used gray Plymouth, and we headed home to Kentucky. His parents, Richard and Era, were so relieved to have him home. They had already accepted me as a part of the family and were ready to help us plan a wedding.

Richard had purchased the old commissary building in Pike Floyd Hollow and used the lumber for the construction of a building where he and Walter could open a business. He was an agent for the C & O Railway but had time to oversee the work and have it ready. It lacked a few finishing touches, especially the upstairs apartment where we would live.

We worked together to finish the job and set our wedding date for June 5. It never entered my mind to want a real wedding gown. They were for big church weddings and we wanted a small one. I did buy a special dress that I thought was beautiful, but in looking at our wedding pictures later, I decided it looked better on the rack than it did on me. At that stage, Walter would have thought I was pretty if I were dressed in burlap.

Wedding Bells

Our wedding was at his parents' home with our beloved Preacher Stratton performing the ceremony. My friend Anna Layne was maid of honor and Walter's Marine buddy Shelbert Maynard was best man. Walter's sister Betty played the piano, and our favorite high school teacher Carlos Hale Haywood sang, "I'll Be Loving You Always."

Several family members and a few close friends attended. Sylvia and Buford were there, along with my dear Aunt Lillie. Walter's Aunt Gustava was there too, and her daughter, Addie Bea, filled out our marriage certificate.

We went to Savannah Beach, Georgia, for our honeymoon and rented a cottage by the ocean. It was my first time at the beach. One afternoon I was wearing a two-piece bathing suit and, as we played in the surf, a wave hit me with such force my top came off. I jumped up and down calling for Walter to come help me, and he was laughing so hard I had trouble understanding his orders to, "Get under the water!"

We lived with Richard and Era the short while it took to finish our apartment, and it was fun choosing wallpaper and adding the finishing touches. With the war just ended, there was no new furniture to be found. Manufacturers had switched from building furniture to making supplies for the war effort, and nothing new had been made for months. Had it been available, we couldn't afford it. We found a used bed, stove, table and chairs. Every furnishing we had was used, but no mansion could have suited us any better than those four rooms and a bath over the store. We were together.

Walter and his dad named the business R. L. Hall & Son Furniture Company. The whole concept of operating a business was new to Walter and it would take them both to get it off the ground. There wasn't enough furniture available to stock it fully, so they decided to add groceries in one side of the building. They made every effort to stock it with merchandise people of the area needed most.

In November of that year, Sylvia married Fred Hall, an Army veteran, and he moved in with her, Jewel and Buford. About two weeks later, Jewel came to our apartment crying. "What's wrong?" I asked.

"I have to quit school and get a job," she cried. "Fred told me he married my sister, not the whole family. I have to find somewhere else to live."

"Well, you just found it," I told her. We have an extra bedroom and we'll go get your clothes." She was concerned that Walter might not approve, but he assured her she was very much wanted at our house. The arrangement was better for her anyway since she was a high school senior and we lived only a mile from school. We enjoyed every day of having her, attending ball games to see her cheerlead and music programs where she was the soloist. Upon graduation, she was awarded a scholarship to the Conservatory of Music in Cincinnati. After studying there for several months, she returned home to marry Dean Conn, her high school sweetheart.

A cause for worry and sadness crept into our lives like a thief. Richard was diagnosed with stomach cancer. Whatever else we wanted to do, helping him overcome the illness became a priority. His employer, the C & O Railway, had specialists at their hospital in Huntington, and he received the best care they could provide. The new business was a real boost to his morale, and the days Walter drove him for treatments were special times for father and son to talk.

The store was going pretty well and Richard resigned his job with the railway. I didn't know how to cook when we married, but Era gave me some pointers and I worked at it. When I served meals, they ate as though it was a real treat and no one said a discouraging word.

Richard and Era lived just back of the store, and when business was slow, I'd run over to see them. When Richard saw me coming, he remarked to anyone in earshot, "Here comes little bird legs."

Some days he didn't feel like going to the store so I visited him, and we spent hours talking of things we both cared about. I'd never known a father like Richard. He was so thoughtful of me and understood my wish to do well. Walter was usually busy with the store, and I had the feeling Richard sometimes talked to him through me. He knew that whatever I learned I would share.

He taught me about human nature and dealing with people. "You want to be fair with everyone," he said, "but some people will lead you out on limb if you let them. Most people trade on credit, and because they give you their business, some will think you might give them a loan. The first time you do it, they'll repay it and all is good. Then you do it again. After a time, you'll loan them money they can't repay. They'll feel embarrassed and quit trading with you, and you've not only lost your money, you've lost their business too." I loved his teaching.

There wasn't anything I couldn't talk to Richard about, and one day I shared that I wanted to have a baby. I weighed all of 105 pounds and I guess he thought my chances were as slim as I was, but he grinned a little and heard me out. As weeks went by, he casually asked now and then, "Any sign of that baby yet?" I would have to tell him, "No, not yet, but I'm hoping."

Betty had married John Porter and when their first child, John Richard, was born I became even more anxious. One day I came bouncing in and announced, "I really think it's going to happen. I got me a bottle of Cardui tonic, and they tell me there's a baby in every bottle!"

I'd never seen him laugh so hard. He finally got his composure and said, "Honey, I know you're trying but, I declare, I'm afraid they've missed your bottle."

Chapter 17
We Gain, We Lose

You wouldn't think morning sickness would be something to jubilate over, but I was delighted. I ate breakfast three times one morning as it kept coming back up. Dr. Frank Vernon confirmed the news I was so anxious to hear. I was going to have a baby!

I asked if he had any special instructions and he said, "No, just try not to fall down." I went directly to G. C. Murphy's store in Pikeville and bought a tiny undershirt and socks and brought them for Walter to see. He was excited too, but he had customers at the store and I couldn't wait to tell Richard and Era.

Before I got all the way through the door, I was squealing, "It worked! My tonic worked! I'm going to have a baby!" They laughed and hugged me and made me feel as if it was the best news they had ever heard.

It was a cold February day and, going home again, I had to walk down a little snow-covered slope. My feet flew right out from under me and I landed on my bottom - the only thing Dr. Vernon told me not to do!

We Gain, We Lose

Time passed quickly and the cold winter turned to spring, then summer. Our upstairs apartment wasn't air conditioned and one day I took a bath three times just to keep cool. Another day I kept slicing off a little piece of watermelon from the cooler till I'd eaten the whole thing.

When Walter returned from making deliveries, he was ready for a snack and walked to the cooler. "What happened to the watermelon?" he asked. I said, "I ate it."

He was alarmed that eating a whole watermelon might affect our baby, but May Crum assured him, "It won't hurt either of them. If that's what she wanted, it won't hurt her."

May was right. Our little girl arrived safe and sound, August 30, 1948. We gave her my mother's first name and Richard's second, calling her Nancy Lee. No child was ever more wanted or more loved. She was my treasure to have and to hold, and now we were a family.

Nancy was born with allergies that made life rough for her. We kept experimenting with different formulas but they all gave her what everyone called "the colic." She cried and cried and I rocked and patted and sang, comforting her the best I could.

We knew very little of allergies and didn't understand how sick they were making her. One night, at the age of five months, her temperature shot to 103. We rushed her to a doctor who was an old school friend, and he put her in the hospital. For a few days, her temperature was down in the morning but back up in the afternoon. We were really worried. I overheard two nurses talking, and it terrified me. I said, "Walter, they think she's going to die!"

We were already concerned that we should have taken her to a more experienced doctor and Walter left immediately to go find Dr. Vernon in Pikeville. He said, "Walter, I ought to kick your ass! Go get that baby right now!"

We didn't even tell the staff we were leaving – we just bundled her up and headed to the hospital in Pikeville. We made a brief stop for Richard and Era to see her as he'd been too sick to come to the hospital. He held her briefly and, as he kissed her head, I saw a tear roll down his pale cheek.

Nancy was diagnosed with viral pneumonia, and Dr. Vernon worked frantically to save her life. She soon began responding to treatment and, after a few days, we were able to bring her home. We were anxious to give her the best of care, but it took time to learn the treatment she needed most. An optician finally directed us to an allergist. As we cared for Nancy, Richard was losing ground. Nothing we did seemed to help.

In the same year we opened the store, a new post office was established for the community of Mare Creek. We were urged to apply for it and set up quarters in a part of the store, but that meant I would have to serve as postmaster and I didn't want to do that. My idea of a postmaster was a little man in suspenders and I didn't fit the mold. Ballard Clark was the first applicant for the job and had no competition, but he found it too confining and the pay too meager. He resigned.

Walter's uncle Aaron Conn then took the job but decided it wasn't for him either. People were concerned that the office might close and Richard urged me to take the job. He said it would be good for store business, so I finally agreed.

This was a political appointment and I needed a recommendation from my congressman. I was the first such appointee of Carl Perkins, who was newly elected to Congress.

The day I became a postmaster, April 27, 1949, I was twenty-two years old and had never been inside a post office. Mr. Biteman, the inspector who installed me, looked so stern he scared me to half to death. But before he left me with the stamps, money orders and a book of regulations, I asked, "Would you please come back tomorrow?" He gave me a firm, "No, I don't have time to come back tomorrow. Just read your instructions and you'll do all right." Fortunately, it was a learn-as-you-go job and I didn't have to know it all at once.

The old inspector wouldn't have known how to train me for what I would encounter. On my second day at work, I sold a woman four stamps at five cents each. She handed them back to me with her letters and said, "You put them on. I don't like to lick the things." I responded, "You think I do?"

A few customers ordered baby chicks by mail and had them shipped COD. If they changed their minds or couldn't come up with the money, I was stuck with them for the day and had to listen to them "cheep." A few usually died in transit, making them smell as if they all had died. If the customer didn't claim them before closing time, I had to auction them to the highest bidder.

The biggest part of the job was exchanging outgoing and incoming mail at the train station. It wasn't hard to toss a First Class mail pouch onto the train, but all the rest was tied in a canvas sack. I weighed just over a hundred pounds so I sometimes needed help swinging a heavy mail sack on board.

The train station served three offices – Betsy Layne, Justell and Mare Creek. The train had a schedule but was rarely on time so we three postmasters just chatted while we waited. If our customers saw the post office doors closed, they understood the train was late.

The post office was open eight hours a day except for the time spent waiting for the train. But any time I was at the store, I was happy to open the office to get a customer's mail. There were no mail boxes – just general delivery. I was the only government employee in our community and my salary was $48 a month – and that included rent for the facility.

As I coped with my little dilemmas, Richard's condition was worsening. He had no appetite, the pain intensified and he was spending more time in the hospital. Nothing was helping. Sylvia helped me care for Nancy so I could be a nurse, either at home or the hospital. Dr. Vernon taught me to give him morphine shots so he could be home more. It took all of us to provide his care – Era, Betty, John, Walter and me. We were there in all the ways we knew to make him comfortable. Despite the best care we could give him, he lost his battle with cancer on November 3, 1949.

He was more than a father-in-law to me. He was the best father I'd ever known. No one was more devastated than I when he left us.

Chapter 18
Feathering Out

It was a good while before Walter could bear to take his father's name off their signs. Eventually he changed the name of the business from R. L. Hall and Son to Hall Furniture Company. The business grew steadily and he hired Hydrac Harmon to help run it.

Any time we prospered a little and got something new, Walter said we "feathered out." In 1950, we got our first new car, a pretty blue Buick Special.

While living with David and his family in California, Buford joined the Marines. He called one night to say he was being sent to Korea. Two days later we were on the road heading toward the west coast. Sylvia, Graham and Era went with us, and Nancy who was not quite two, made six of us in the new Buick.

Feathering Out

It was a wonderful eighteen-day trip. We took a northern route going out, by way of the Rocky Mountains and Yellowstone Park, and came back across the Mojave Desert, by the Hoover Dam and into Grand Canyon. We didn't have super highways to travel, but it was fun. Walter and Graham took turns driving. We could all take little naps as we were moving – that is, all but Sylvia. When the car stopped, she'd fall asleep, but as soon as we were back in gear, she'd wake up again. She enjoyed the trip, but it wore her out.

Back at work, I was asked to join the National Association of Postmasters (NAPUS). One of the most important gatherings of the organization is the state convention. I missed the first one because Nancy was too little to take and I wouldn't leave her. The next year, 1952, the convention was held at Kentucky Dam Village in Gilbertsville. Nancy was now three and a half and it was easy to talk Walter into going with us because of the chance to fish Kentucky Lake. He attended the evening functions with us and spent the days fishing while Nancy and I attended meetings. She was content to play with a toy rabbit and was no problem at all. The Louisville Courier Journal ran an article in their magazine about that gathering and featured me as the youngest postmaster there. A picture of Nancy and me accompanied the story.

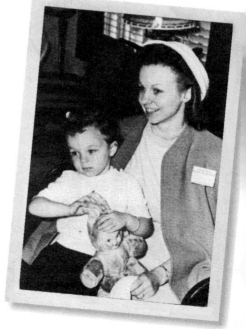

Feathering Out

We didn't know while at that convention that we had another baby on the way. I hadn't bought any more tonics to help the cause, but the news excited us almost as much as the first time and we started making plans again. We had no idea about the baby's sex and would speculate about it. We wondered before Nancy was born too, and Walter observed, "I want one thing understood. Whether it's girl or boy, if you're teaching or correcting it, I'll never disagree with you in front of the child. And if I'm the one doing the correcting, you'd better not!" We laughed that day but realized how important it was. We agreed that, if we had one or a dozen, we'd remember to practice that rule.

My due date was near and Christmas approaching when I went to see Dr. Vernon one winter day. He said, "It can be any time now, but you may drag around till Christmas day." He gave me some quinine and castor oil and said, "Take this just before you go to bed tonight, and I'll see you soon." Era stayed with us to be with Nancy in case we left in the night, and about 5:00 that next morning, I knew we should be going. That first labor had lasted a night and a day, and I thought it would again. Jewel went with us and Sylvia would come later. When Sylvia arrived about 9:00 a.m., I said, "Isn't she pretty!" Our new baby girl was already there.

Rhonda Gale was born December 21, 1952. She weighed 5 lbs., 11 oz., and seemed a perfect fit in Walter's hands as he held her. We brought her home from the hospital on Christmas Eve, and she would be our

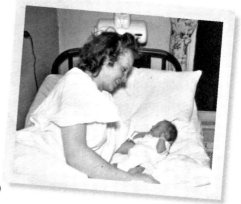

year-round Christmas present. Nancy regarded her as "our baby" and was never jealous, and Era, Sylvia and May Crum helped us care for them. Those were good years as we worked and loved and wound our lives together with many others.

From the time she could walk, Rhonda adored her father. If he decided to take a nap on the couch, he could brace for her to climb over him till he gave up and played with her. She was a little blonde bundle of energy. Nancy was quieter and less demanding but from the time he first saw them, he adored both his girls. Having two babies made our four-room apartment seem a little crowded, and we began making plans for a house. We bought a nice lot for building and started shopping for house plans, but it would take a little more "feathering out" to start a house.

It was wonderful being a family. We were green about parenting, but whatever we lacked in know-how, we made up for in our zeal to give them our best. We weren't so concerned about material abundance, but wanted to instill those qualities that make for happiness and to give them the security of knowing they were wanted and loved.

I was like a mother hen, concerned with their physical care. I wanted to cook what they liked, and enjoyed buying pretty little dresses and shoes. They especially loved a new Easter dress each year and shopping for them was a big deal. The ones we chose were their "Easter dresses" all year. It might be September when one of them would ask, "Can I wear my Easter dress?" Once Rhonda was playing in a little short dress, and I saw she'd left her panties off. "Get your bloomers on!" I squealed. She laughed and repeated, "Get my boonies on!" Their underpants were always boonies after that.

Walter especially enjoyed finding things to do to make life fun for them. He planned regular vacations every year and often came up with overnight camping trips, drive-in movies, games, pets and simple treats. I often thought about losing my own mother so early, and of my father's subsequent inattention and prayed that we could both be there to get them grown up. One night before we went to sleep I said, "Walter, if I die before you and you don't take good care of our girls, I'm going to sit on the headboard of your bed and haunt you." He laughed that wonderful laugh and asked, "Are you really worried about that?"

And I needn't have worried, for I could have been jealous of the bond between them. There was nothing the girls couldn't – or wouldn't – talk to their daddy about, and he cared about every facet of their lives. Before they were half grown, I realized they would always care for each other – and I could forget about the haunting.

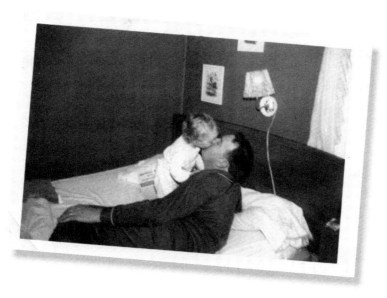

Chapter 19
Moving on up

During my very first days of riding the school bus, I noticed everything new – the different students at each stop and the scenery along the way. As we drew closer to school one day I could see something being built and asked, "What's going on there?" Mary Dotson had the answer, "My dad said Dr. Chandler is building a real nice house out there."

Years later, after we had become parents, Walter and I got to know Dr. Chandler and his family. We lived within a quarter of a mile from them, and it was wonderful having a doctor nearby. Sometimes he made house calls to our apartment, and sometimes we came to the office beside his house. He was a congenial fellow we came to trust and appreciate, but after he gave Rhonda her first injection, she bawled and squalled at the sight of him. If I asked Nancy not to cry, she just bit her lip and took it. He said, "I declare, it hurts me to give this child a shot. I know it hurts, and I think I'd feel better if she cried."

Moving on up

The Chandlers had a small garden, some apple trees and a grape arbor, and one evening he was trimming some of the grape vines when he had a fatal heart attack. We were so sorry to lose him, for we thought of him as a real friend.

Mrs. Chandler continued to shop at our store and one afternoon she announced, "I'm moving to South Carolina to be near my son, and I'd like to sell you my house." We had already bought a nice lot to build on and were looking at plans for the ranch style house we thought we wanted. Besides, we didn't think we could afford her house with all the property that went with it. But every time she came to the store she mentioned how much she wanted us to come and see her place. Then one day she insisted, "Children, if you're going to look at my house, you'll need to come this afternoon. I'm going away tomorrow and won't be back for a while." Mostly as a courtesy, Walter said, "All right, Mrs. Chandler, we'll be up in a little while."

The white two-story house, framed by beautiful trees, sat four hundred feet back from the road with almost that much distance in the back. We had been so reluctant to even look, but the minute we stepped through the door, we fell in love. The living room felt spacious and elegant in contrast to our small four-room apartment. The house had hardwood floors and gleaming woodwork crafted from California Redwood. Arched doorways led to a formal dining room that circled around to a kitchen with a breakfast bar. Adjacent to the kitchen was a sunny breakfast room with huge windows. For a couple that had hosted large groups of friends and family in such small quarters, the idea of so much space was almost unbelievable.

Moving on up

The bank granted us a loan to buy the house and gave us a little payment book. They returned it to us each time showing how our payment was applied. The very first one showed that half was principle and half was interest.

"Walter," I wailed, " Look at this! Half went for interest! We'll never in this world get our house paid for." It turned out to be the best business deal we ever made.

As soon as we got our furniture arranged enough to cook and set a table, we invited good friends from church, Clifford and Winnie Boyd and their two girls, Sue and Lana, to dinner. It was Walter's idea. "I want them with us to ask God's blessing on this house," he said. Those blessings have abounded through the years, in good measure, pressed down, shaken together and running over.

Nancy was six and Rhonda two when we moved and Nancy immediately claimed the upstairs bedroom. Rhonda had her own room too but she preferred slipping upstairs to sleep in Nancy's bed. Both girls were excited to have such a huge lawn and their special playhouse that had been Dr. Chandler's office. After living in an upstairs apartment all their lives, they were like little birds set free.

We now had room for the pets we could never have before, but there was no way to predict the motley array that would make their way through our doors and our hearts. There were kittens willing to be dressed in doll clothes, a rambunctious duck named Quack, a pretty pony the girls called Princess, a special little bulldog named Bud, and a young beagle whose first attempts to bark sounded more like crowing and earned him the name Rooster.

Excited and anxious as I was to move into the new house, I was surprised by the feeling of sadness I had about

Moving on up

leaving our cozy little apartment. It was where we'd spent the first nine years of our lives together and learned we really could make it on our own.

Many special people came to share those first happy days. Richard and Era were in and out, Delilah came from Detroit several times, relatives traveling from one point to another stopped over, and May Crum made it her second home. Several members of our family had lived with us. For a while it was Jewel, then Graham, Kenneth and Buford. We loved every minute of having them and never once felt crowded.

It's likely that first decade would have been much the same in any setting, but this apartment had been a wonderful beginning for us. It's where we lived when our children were born and we became a real family. It's where I learned, in some degree, how to cook and keep house, and where Walter became adept at managing a business.

It's also where I learned how nice it was to sleep with my head on his shoulder.

Chapter 20
Parenting

Our children were our pride and joy. No other good fortune compared with the feeling of having our own family. We were as green as grass about raising children, but what we lacked in parenting skills was compensated by our zeal to do well and we learned as we went along.

I know now that Nancy was an unusual child in that she was well-behaved from the beginning. When we told her she couldn't do something, she believed she couldn't do it and didn't argue. I taught her nice manners and, if we were all going out, I'd just explain that we'd be seeing a lot of people and I could rely on her to make us proud.

Since she was our first, I thought all children were like Nancy. If a child threw a tantrum in a public place, I thought it was a shame the parents hadn't taught proper behavior. And if one should be rude in any way, I didn't blame the child at all. The parents just hadn't given proper instructions. I was feeling pretty competent about our abilities as parents. Then we had Rhonda.

She was a contradiction to every concept I had about parenting. When she grew enough to walk and talk, there was no predicting which way she would go or what she might say. There were a few lines she knew not to cross, but we learned to stay braced for whatever she might do next.

Unlike her sister, when we took Rhonda out to dinner, we could expect to make a few apologies. If we didn't keep a close watch, she might wind up under the table, in the kitchen or at somebody else's table. Once, in a department store, I thought she was right behind me when I overheard one of the clerks ask another, "Who is that little girl in the stockroom?" Without even looking around to see if she was gone, I headed to get her.

Rhonda's behavior made me appreciate solid little Nancy more and brought me a bit more humility. Quite often I overheard Walter say, "Now, if you can just keep both feet on the ground for a while..."

John Porter gave the girls a pet duck they named Quack. They had a great time with it. They put it in the bathtub to watch it swim and, when it got out, they squealed with laughter watching it shake its tail. They put it in and out of the tub just to see it shake until they wore it out.

Walter Collins thought Quack looked lonesome and brought her a mate. We could have named him Chomp for he would slip up behind us and bite our legs. We could have done without the mate for it taught Quack to be mean, and we had to give them both away. But there was always an array of pets to cope with and care for.

On Nancy's first day of school, she wouldn't let me wait with her for the school bus. She felt very grown up catching the bus with her cousin John Richard. I stood watching from our upstairs window and, when the bus pulled out, I saw three teachers in a car right behind it. They'd seen me dab my eyes and were laughing at me.

Nancy got the common childhood diseases that first year – measles, mumps and chicken-pox – and brought them home to Rhonda. I had my hands full caring for both at the same time.

Rhonda was about five when one of the neighbors said to her, "Honey, it's a shame you're not the little boy your daddy wanted." We didn't know what had happened when our bouncy little girl set out to be her daddy's boy and wanted to trade her pretty dresses for jeans, but it was obvious she had a campaign going. When Walter found out about the remark, he was touched by Rhonda's devotion but furious that such a comment had been made.

He saw how serious she was when he took her fishing in the river one afternoon. While he gathered up a cooler and some "pogie bait" snacks, she had me pin her long hair up under an old cap.

When they got to the river, she insisted on baiting her own hook and they fished a while before deciding to have a snack. When he put a sardine on a cracker for himself, she wanted one too. He saw a little shiver when she put it in her mouth and wasn't surprised that one was enough.

He was casting from the front of the boat and she sat near the back with her line in the water. From the corner of his eye, he saw her spit in the river. With his back toward her, he started talking. "You know, Shug, I've figured something out. I think God knows us better than we know ourselves."

"What do you mean, Daddy?"

"Well," he continued, "I used to think I wanted a son. But then, you and Nancy came along. Now I understand what God knew all along -- I couldn't possibly love a little boy more than I do my girls."

Parenting

When he turned to look at her again, she'd taken off her cap and let her curls hang loose.

Rhonda's first school year was just a week away when one night she came to climb in bed with us. I took her back to her bed and lay with her a while but, when I went back, she was right behind me. This time she said, "My stomach hurts," and I checked her temperature. Sure enough, she had a fever.

I called Dr. Cassady's office the next morning and the nurse said, "Bring her in and we'll check her." A quick test showed the problem and Dr. Cassady said, "Get her up to the hospital. She has appendicitis." I didn't have long to be frantic for he operated that afternoon.

The first get-well cards she got were from her Grandmother and aunts, and each had a dollar bill enclosed. When she got one that was just a card, she looked bewildered, asking "Where's the money?"

Two years later, she got an ear infection that Dr. Wilson in Pikeville was treating. It was a stubborn case that would get better for a while, then flare up again. We were vacationing in Tennessee when she laid her head on my lap and said, "Mommy, I feel bad." She felt hot and, when I touched the left side of her head, she cried out in pain.

The area behind her ear wasn't just red, it was swollen and dark purple! I called Dr. Wilson at home and he detected how scared I was. "Should we bring her home tonight?" I asked, but he said, "No, I have a friend in Knoxville who is an ENT specialist. I want you to see him in the morning. I need his opinion."

We were at his office when it opened the next morning, and it didn't take long for him to confirm the problem was serious. The infection had gotten into the mastoid bone. "She has to have surgery right away," he said. "The closest place that can do it is Children's Hospital in Cincinnati.

The surgery took eight hours. The bone had to be chiseled away – a slow and delicate procedure. Walter paced the hallways and nurses teased him that he wore the floor out. I mostly sat and wrung my hands and asked God to help the doctors. The surgery went well and we brought her home in about a week.

Our dinner times were even more special with all four of us back together again. Each of us was very different, but we were a compatible bunch and there was always laughter and lively conversations around our dinner table.

Walter thought little surprises were important, and he wanted the girls to learn something in whatever they did. One day he told Rhonda he'd heard about a pony for sale and asked if she'd like to go with him to look at it. She was so excited he had to remind her again to "keep both feet on the floor." As they drove along he explained the importance of keeping a poker face when trying to negotiate a business deal. "Now when you see this pony, I don't want you to say a word until we can talk in private. Got that?"

"Got it."

When the man walked out with a beautiful pony, Rhonda squealed, "Oh, Daddy, she's perfect! I love her!" Walter just looked at her and said, "Get in the truck." She was one subdued little girl on the way home.

The two of them went pony shopping several more times but were disappointed with the ones they found. Then one afternoon they found a pretty red one with white feet. He saw the excitement dance in her eyes and she squeezed his hand tightly but didn't say a word. When the man asked her if she liked it, she said, "It's all right, I guess." Walter thought he would burst in not being able to laugh in front of her, but he had made his point. She had no idea how funny it was to him or how much he enjoyed buying the pony she named Princess.

Nancy was quieter and more reserved than Rhonda, keeping her opinions to herself until she was asked. She was always a good student, excelling in many areas including music. At sixteen, she became the pianist and youth choir director at our church. Like my sister Sylvia, she always seemed to know what to do and how to do it. If I worked late, I came home to find dinner on the table. When I traveled, she kept the house running smoothly. She even packed for the whole family when we went on vacations.

Sometimes Walter and I would playfully check how the girls would choose between us. I'd say, "Nancy, I think this, and your daddy thinks that. What do you say?" Always the diplomat, she answered, "You'll have to figure it out yourself. I'm not getting involved."

But if we asked Rhonda the same thing, she didn't have to hear the whole question. She just replied, "Daddy's right."

It was no secret, then or ever, that she was her father's child. Having missed that experience myself, I thought it was pretty nice.

Chapter 21
Store Business

Our customers at the store were some of the most colorful characters we'd ever known. They were the reason our business succeeded and we loved them as our extended families. Rufus and Sudie Wallace had two children, Grady and Anna Sue. "Rube," as we called him, had been burned in a mine explosion and, in his retirement, liked to loaf at the store. His observations about any situation kept the other customers entertained.

Grady also came often to enjoy a Coke and a candy bar. We watched him play basketball at Betsy Layne High School, little dreaming he would play college ball for the South Carolina Gamecocks and is, so far, the only person from our area ever voted All-American.

An old man named "Dad" Canterbury lived in the head of Mare Creek and rode a horse to get his groceries. He told stories about his romance with his wife that kept Walter in stitches. Had they shared the humor with me, maybe I could relate – but they didn't and maybe I couldn't.

Another couple was Sarah and Bee Hunt who had ten children and 37 grandchildren. A normal day for Sarah was hoeing corn for half a day, cooking dinner for her big family then walking the five mile round trip to the store. Since she couldn't carry much at a time, she made the trip almost every day. She chewed tobacco and liked Pepsi warm or cold. When she went to hoe corn, she hid her Pepsi under her bed so Bee wouldn't drink it. She could have saved herself the trouble for he had his own bottle of a different sort stashed away and wasn't interested in hers. Sarah and Walter swapped stories and enjoyed each other until she died at the age of ninety.

Our closest neighbors were May and Clarence Crum who lived just across the road. Clarence worked in the mines and left home early in the morning. By the time we opened the store, May had her housework done, her children off to school and was ready to come and spend the day with us. She came to visit before we had children but, after Nancy was born, she'd say, "I just had to come see this baby!" She enjoyed helping with both girls and, years later, she heard someone talking about Walter Hall's girls. When she expressed some interest, they asked, "Do you know them?"

"Know them?" she exclaimed. "I reckon I do – I've half raised them!"

Our customers weren't the only colorful people we knew. Before Paul and Elaine Gearheart bought the telephone company, his grandmother, Olga Roberts, owned it. She was also the operator and connected us for long distance calls. Our telephone was a crank-type and we had a code for our ring. As the business grew, Walter wanted stationery printed and a sign on his truck with the company's name, address and phone number. So he called Mrs. Roberts to ask, "What's my phone number?"

"Don't you know?" she answered, "Your ring is a long and two shorts."

"I know what my ring is, but my suppliers are asking for a number."

She said, "Well, Honey, what number do you want?"

"It really doesn't matter, Mrs. Roberts. I just need a number."

"Then what number do you like?"

He finally said, "Well, I like ten well enough."

"That's fine," she told him, "then ten can be your number. I'll not let anyone else have it."

So he bought the stationery and had a sign painted on his truck that read: Hall Furniture Company – Mare Creek, Kentucky – Phone: 10.

I'd never liked having Mare Creek as an address. When Walter won a trip to Miami and Havana, we were with a whole group of people and kept being introduced as Mr. and Mrs. Hall from Mare Creek, while others were from Charleston, Georgetown and other such cities. I thought it indicated we were from "way back" and felt that being so young and unworldly was enough to keep us humble. We were already the youngest couple in the group; after seven years in business, he was 27 and I was 26.

As postmaster, I set out to get the name changed and enlisted the help of Carl Perkins, our congressman. I wanted a name of some significance and chose Stanley as it was the name of the first family to settle there. But there was already a Stanley. We finally came up with the variation of Stanville. Anyone who doesn't like the name can blame me.

Store Business

Having both the store and post office to care for was pretty confining, but neither of us ever minded working. One day Walter went to Huntington to buy furniture, leaving me to care for it all. Era came to help me, but after a while she became drowsy and I suggested she go take a nap. I promised to call if I needed her, and she wasn't hard to convince.

I was rearranging some items on a shelf when I looked up to see a total stranger walk in. I'd never seen anyone who even faintly resembled him, and I had no idea where he came from. I was gripped with fear. My hands started shaking, and my voice trembled as I said, "Good afternoon." There wasn't another customer in sight, and I began wishing Era hadn't left. From my days at Greenfield's, I was accustomed to talking with strangers. There had been people of different backgrounds and nationalities, but I'd always been able to find some common subject, if only the weather. But suddenly I didn't trust myself to talk at all.

He spoke very softly, "Ma'am, could you give me something to eat? I haven't eaten today."

I showed him the meat case and asked him to choose from lunch meats as I opened a loaf of bread. I made a couple of sandwiches and got a soft drink from the cooler. Then I showed him where the cakes and candy bars were and said, "Help yourself to whatever you'd like."

He sat down and was eating so hurriedly I knew he must really be hungry. I tried to appear casual as I stepped to the phone and called for Era. "Are you ready to come back?"

"Is something wrong?" she asked, but I couldn't even answer. I heard her say, "I'll be right there."

The man finished eating and thanked me, and I did have presence of mind to say, "You're welcome. Did you have enough?" But I didn't insist on anything more.

As he walked out the door and turned left, Era came up from the right. She saw him walk away and said, "Did you see that poor man's feet with those big holes in his socks?"

What she said startled me and I grabbed some money from the cash register and hurried to catch him. He would surely need to eat again, and I hadn't even thought of that. I dashed out the door – but he was gone! There had been no traffic in either direction and no house he could have entered in the few short seconds. He was just gone.

The following day, I asked all our customers if they'd seen a strange man in the neighborhood, but no one had. Even May Crum, who lived across the road and saw everything, hadn't seen him.

Sometime later I read the Bible admonition: "Be not forgetful to entertain strangers: for thereby some have entertained angels unawares." (Hebrews 13:2) Since then, I've believed that happened to me – that an angel became visible to me for that brief encounter. I've never understood why I was so afraid, and I've wished so much I'd been more hospitable.

But who would expect an angel to appear physically hungry – or have holes in his socks?

Chapter 22
Wipe Out

We bought the house in 1955, and in 1957 we had a flood that almost washed the Big Sandy valley off the map. It was the worst to hit this area in more than 100 years. As the water came up, our neighbors called us at the store to say their house was being flooded and they were at ours. "Just make yourselves at home," we told them. "We have to stay here and salvage what we can."

The water came up fast. We took the children to May Crum's house on a hill and it seemed the whole neighborhood was there. Before we could move anything from the store to higher ground, Walter was asked to bring a boat to rescue stranded people. Realizing the post office would be flooded, I stayed behind cramming all the mail, record books and other important items into a large mail sack. By the time he came back for me, the water was already two feet deep and I was standing on top of my desk clutching the big canvas sack. Debris was floating all around but it never entered my mind to be afraid. I just trusted him to rescue me from the rising water. He drove the boat through the big double doors into the building, then removed his pants and shoes, climbed out and carried me to safety.

When the water crested, it was about eight feet deep in the store building -- almost to the ceiling. The business had been completely stocked with furniture, appliances, groceries and supplies and we lost it all. The foul and muddy scene that remained was all consuming and we worked until we were numb trying to clean it up.

Flood water had gone completely through the ceiling at the home of our neighbors, the Furman family. One of their daughters was a medical missionary in Sierra Leone and another was away teaching school, but the couple and three of their children lived with us for five weeks. Water had come into our house too, but only an inch deep – just enough to keep them stranded upstairs for a while and buckle our beautiful hardwood floors.

The cleanup task was overwhelming. By the end of each day, we were exhausted and could see so little progress. I remember sitting on our back steps and crying at supper time. We had worked from dawn to dusk for days and days and it still seemed that everything we touched had mud on it.

I was dressed in blue jeans and boots cleaning the post office when Loren Gard, a postal official from Cincinnati, came by with a carload of critical supplies. He was making rounds in an effort to get area post offices operating again. He was pleased to learn that I'd saved records, but I was a desolate sight in the mess that was my office.

Fortunately, the Red Cross moved in to help families, and a loan from the Small Business Administration enabled us to re-stock the store. As soon as we received new inventory, our customers were ready to buy.

Things slowly dried out and fell into place, but the subtle pervasive smell of flood mud would never quite leave the store building. You just learned to live with it.

* * * ***

In 1964, I learned that Morehead College was offering evening classes in Prestonsburg. One course that caught my eye was "Writing and Public Speaking." I had to do a little of both in my job, so I enrolled. I thoroughly enjoyed the class and earned 3 hours of college credit. Walter always said I had two hours and forty-five minutes.

With the housing shortage in our region, Walter saw an opportunity and added a line of mobile homes to his business. On one of his buying trips, he stopped by a boat dealership in Charleston, West Virginia, "just to look." He always loved the water and, even when we could barely pay for utilities, he had a boat of some kind. The first ones were required to do little more than float but, as we feathered out, he traded up.

He fell in love with a boat he found in Charleston and the salesman promised to hold it for two days. He was as excited as I'd ever seen him when he took me back with him two days later to buy it. But the man had not kept his word. He'd sold the boat and Walter was furious. He considered his word his bond and expected the same from others.

In spite of being angry, Walter still wanted the boat. He found out where they were manufactured and went to the factory in Sanford, Florida. He must have impressed the company officials with his enthusiasm, for they asked him to consider being a dealer. That opened up a whole new world for us. Fishing boats, runabouts and cabin cruisers would soon lead to luxury houseboats. His love of the water made the boating business for him like throwing a rabbit in the briar patch. He had found his element.

From the time he brought in the first houseboat, we kept a demonstrator on Dewey Lake and we made his occupation our recreation. In fact, we would not be without a houseboat for the next 38 years. Our boats, like that little four room apartment, were made for sharing.

Chapter 23
Getting Involved

I was so impressed by the 1952 convention that I didn't want to miss another. The next was in Middlesboro, and I made it a priority to get there, though Rhonda was only five months old. My sister Jewel took her daughter Sherry with us and cared for the children as I attended meetings.

The following year, the convention was held at Cumberland Falls, but both of my girls had the measles and I couldn't take them or leave them. It was the only one I missed during a thirty-seven year career. I was appointed Floyd County chairman for our state chapter, and in two more years, was elected district director to work with the state officers as a contact person for four counties.

After fourteen years on a job I had twice refused, the work had become more interesting. When Postmaster Add Boyd of our neighboring town announced his retirement in 1963, I applied for his job and was transferred to the larger office. It meant more responsibility and more work, but more pay.

Getting Involved

In that same year, state convention was scheduled to be at Jenny Wiley State Park, just fourteen miles from home. Bess May of Prestonsburg would be Host Postmaster, but I was asked to assist her with local planning. I'd never worked on a planning committee of any kind, but I was ready and willing.

Bess was a gracious lady but a little reserved, so she asked me to do the talking when we went to seek support from local businesses. Having the convention here was good for the area, and every business we contacted was willing to contribute in some way. When our postmasters arrived, along with visitors and officials from other states, they received a royal welcome.

My brother-in-law John Porter had a car dealership and provided a nice car for transporting official guests. Jack Tomlinson, who owned Kentucky Oil Company and had his own plane, volunteered to pick up guests at bigger airports and bring them to the smaller one in Prestonsburg. Local businesses sent flowers and favors for every luncheon and banquet. School groups and "Miss Kathryn" Frazier's Patsy Teenagers provided entertainment. Whatever our 300 guests would expect in a larger city was provided right here at our state park.

Our state officers didn't know the staff of May Lodge so they used me as the contact person for whatever was needed. If it was an easel for a presentation, an adjustment of the thermostat or whatever anyone wanted, by the second day a common phrase was, "Find Aileen."

When convention ended, the state officers asked what was owed for the different services we had arranged. I said, "I

Getting Involved

didn't know we had access to a budget, so everything was donated." That both surprised and pleased them, and convinced them I was willing and able to get things done. When new officers were elected, I was chosen as one of four Vice Presidents.

Until I transferred to Betsy Layne, Walter and I had worked alongside each other as Hall Furniture and the Stanville post office were in the same building. Being separated for work was good for us as we were more eager to see each other in the evening. Suppertime with our girls was very special as we all shared stories of what had happened to each of us since morning.

Walter was a real story teller and could make the most common event sound funny. Nancy and Rhonda had stories of their own, but if things got a little quiet, one of them would ask, "Well, Mother, what did Miss Mahoney have to say today?" Miss Mahoney was a postal customer who was also a delightful character and a never ending source for stories to share. She had a speech impediment that never dampened her exuberance. She always came through the door asking, "How you doing today, Fweetheart?"

Each year in February, our NAPUS officers went to Washington for a national legislative conference. Postmasters from across the country called on their respective legislators with concerns about the postal service. This was prior to Postal Reform when the Post Office Department was still part of the President's cabinet.

Delma Smith, of Garfield in Breckenridge County, had been State Secretary/Treasurer for fourteen years when NAPUS met in 1967. She was good at the job and could have been re-elected but was offered a management job in the Louisville post office and needed to be replaced.

Without even discussing it with me, the Kentucky group called on Congressman Perkins, and told him they were going to ask me to be a candidate. He said, "If she will agree to run, tell her she'll have my full support."

By the time I was approached, they had already started campaigning for me, but I wasn't sure I wanted the challenge of being secretary for our state's 1,364 offices.

My more experienced friends knew Congressman Perkins was one of the most influential members of Congress. They also knew I would work and would be a great help to the organization. A few others wanted to be secretary so I had some opposition, but I didn't have to campaign much; the others did it for me. I was elected at the June 1967 convention in Owensboro.

Gene Pinson was a postal inspector when Walter and I met him at that first convention fifteen years earlier and, being from Pike County, he seemed to take pride that this postmaster from "back home" was doing well. He had long since become Inspector-in-Charge for the three states that made up the Cincinnati Region, and he always attended our conventions. That night in Owensboro, he called me aside and asked, "Can I give you some advice? You'll be invited many places and to many events. Accept every invitation you can and enjoy the experience."

No advice was ever taken more to heart. The only invitations I didn't accept were those I didn't get. I observed appointments, retirements and funerals, went to state houses and mansions, training rooms and headquarters, always

Getting Involved

aware I was representing postmasters. The region was made up of Indiana, Kentucky and Ohio, dubbed IKO. Each year, we had a three day training institute near Regional Headquarters in Cincinnati, where we could choose courses in Public Relations, Accounting, Office Management, Public Speaking, Diplomacy and various other training to make us more effective. I took advantage of the classes that helped me most.

Travel was an important part of the secretary's office. Our state was made up of twelve districts and each held an annual meeting. I worked with district directors in arranging those meetings, and then attended each one. I wrote letters of invitation to special guests and, with an old typewriter and a hand-cranked copier, sent letters to about 1400 people on a regular basis. We had a state publication called *The Kentuckian*, and I wrote a column for each issue.

For six years, I traveled to almost every town and community in the state, sometimes taking my children, and sometimes going alone. Once I was caught in a blinding snow storm on the Western Kentucky Parkway, alone on an unfamiliar road almost 400 miles from home. When I finally got to Lake Barkley State Park, a few friends were there to meet me and I soon forgot how scared I'd been. Walter said that if I got sick, meeting with three postmasters would make me well.

Carl Perkins seemed pleased to have me serving in a statewide office, but I had no wish to impose on him. I was a little reluctant when a postmaster friend in Jeffersontown asked me to request a recommendation for him for a job at the Washington headquarters. I wrote to Mr. Perkins, explaining that, "This postmaster is not even in your district, but . . ."

That friend spent the rest of his career in Headquarters and never forgot the kindness.

Soon one of my customers asked me to request an appointment for his son to the U. S. Naval Academy. I said, "The Congressman would really rather hear from you about your wish," but he replied, "I've already asked, but I want you to ask too." Again, I called, and the son was accepted. When he left the Academy, he was educated to be a medical doctor.

Another postmaster friend in Knox County wanted an interview arranged for a job with the Postal Inspection Service. By then, we'd gone through Postal Reform and political intervention was discouraged. I reminded him of this until he asked, "Will you ask him or not?" Needless to say, I asked – and he got the job.

The only referral that didn't work out was a postmaster from another district who wanted a job in the Cincinnati Region. It was a time when race relations had become very sensitive, and he was asked how he felt about working with minorities. He said, "I'd have no trouble with that," but then he added, "That doesn't mean I'd want them in my home." That remark killed his chance for a transfer.

It's surprising how close you can get with a group of people when you work together week after week. We became much like family. Jean Hall, Delma Smith and I traveled together so much we could almost read each others minds.

When supporters suggested I run for the office of president of Kentucky NAPUS, it sounded like the wildest dream. I knew I could handle the work for I'd worked closely with five presidents, but the others had all been men from much larger offices. I enjoyed filling whatever role was sent

Getting Involved

my way, and no woman had ever served in the top office. When I agreed to be a candidate, no one opposed me.

It was during the 1971 state convention at Lake Barkley State Park that I was elected the first woman to serve our state as president.

Chapter 24

Family Fun Years

Our years as a young family could be called the springtime of our lives, for everything was new and growing. Every advancement our children made, every new thing they learned was one more discovery to share and be glad for. To us, they were the smartest kids ever.

We were close to other family members and it seemed only natural that we take vacations and spend leisure time together. Betty and John Porter had two children, John Richard and Susan, who were near Nancy and Rhonda's ages, and they were all big buddies. After Richard died, Era married Erman Ratliff, and he was a loving grandfather to all of them.

In the summer of 1956, we rented a big house on Myrtle Beach, South Carolina, for a week long vacation. The children called Era "Mamaw," and they thought it hilarious that she wore two girdles under her bathing suit.

Family Fun Years

When vacation time rolled around, Walter would get up about 6:00 a.m. and go to the foot of the stairs where both girls could hear him and loudly sing, "Vacation comes but once a year, and all it brings is joy and cheer." The girls needed coaxing out of bed on school days, but on this day, Rhonda came bounding from her room and Nancy fairly bounced down the stairs.

We took one overnight camping trip at the lake close to home before we had a tent or adequate supplies. We used furniture pads to sleep on, and we had lanterns that had to have air pumped into them

occasionally to keep them burning. I closed my eyes and was ready to drop off to sleep when I thought I heard something move. I imagined a snake and got up to look around and pump more air into the lanterns. I didn't see anything, but it may as well have been a bear for sleep just would not come.

All was fun for Walter and the girls, and it was play the next morning when he cooked breakfast with makeshift equipment. I bemoaned the fact I had a Beautyrest mattress and an electric stove at home. Even after Walter bought more sophisticated camping gear, we drove two vehicles to the lake for I almost always wanted to come home early.

Bebe and Emmit Conn, our close friends from high school days, also had two children, Steve and Barbie. They went with us and the Porters on one trip and it was so much fun we kept planning vacations together. With three couples and six children, it was sometimes a challenge to get a table for twelve but it was worth the effort.

Each summer, we found a place the whole group liked. The women and children preferred going to the beach, but the men opted for fishing and boating on the lake. Pleasing the children was always a priority, but they had a great time wherever they were and didn't mind alternating.

No one objected when John assumed the role of decision maker. Whether we were going out to dinner or for a week long vacation, he decided where we ate, took rest stops or had fill-ups for our cars. Nobody ever disagreed with John, and he saved us a lot of hassle.

One special vacation was at Nags Head on the Outer Banks of North Carolina where we saw signs urging tourists not to miss the Shipwreck. The kids were having a ball in the pool when Walter insisted they get cleaned up so he could take us all to see it. We got there to find nothing but a post stuck in the ground to indicate where a ship had once wrecked. "Is this it?" everybody grumbled. Walter uttered a profanity and the kids squealed. "Daddy said a bad word!" "Uncle Walter said a bad word!" The grown-ups tried not to laugh while the children giggled and carried on and we were all entertained at his expense.

On another trip to Daytona Beach, we found a new restaurant we wanted to try. We told the guys they had to wear ties and they reluctantly agreed. As we were dressing there was a knock at our door. I opened it and there stood Emmit asking, "Do I look alright?" He was wearing a tie – but no shirt.

During another vacation, we were all at Norris Lake. We spent the morning at the pool and were having lunch when Walter said, "I'd like to take a boat ride and explore the lake. Anybody want to join me?" Emmit said he was ready, and John volunteered, "Why don't you take Aileen and Bebe with you, and Betty and I will take the children out to that trading post by the highway." They loaded all six children into their station wagon and gave each a dollar to spend. The children thought they were in high cotton.

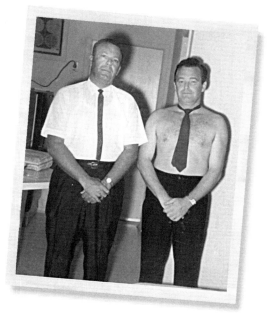

John Richard and Steve bought little leather whips they were proud of and, when Steve saw Nancy's selection, he was shocked. "You got that little old black bear when you could have had a whip? You wasted your dollar!" We all laughed then, and "wasted your dollar" is a phrase we still use to describe any questionable purchase.

Back home again, we prepared for another school year and were back at our jobs with new energy. We were involved with PTA, Band Parents, ball games, recitals, Halloween carnivals and endless activities as chaperones, fund raisers, ticket-takers and just about anything needed until our girls were through high school.

Nancy was 16 and had just gotten her driver's license when someone traded Walter a 1947 Jeepster convertible. He had it painted bright red, put on a new white canvas top and installed a tag with her name on the front. It had a horn that went, "oooga," and it wasn't capable of speeding. When he gave her the keys, she was on top of the world.

One day she and Rhonda attended a parade in Pikeville and it rained, making the streets slick. As they rounded a curve coming out of town, the Jeepster slid into a little tree beside a house. Nancy was really distressed, and Walter went to see the owner to pay for the damages. Seeing the tree very close to the street and all scarred up, he asked the man why he didn't just cut it down. He said, "I can't do that. Someone hits it every time it rains, and it pays too well."

The little Jeepster was really popular and a lot of people wanted to buy it. Walter would sell almost anything he had, but Nancy and her friends were so enamored by it that he wouldn't dare let it go. Around the time she was planning to enroll in college at Prestonsburg, someone traded him a late model turquoise Thunderbird. As soon as Nancy saw it, her love of the Jeepster faded and the T-bird became her vehicle of choice. The Jeepster was parked until Rhonda learned to drive.

Family Fun Years

Before completing her first year at Prestonsburg Community College, Nancy told us she wanted to get married. She promised to go on to school so we finally agreed, but when they told us the date they'd chosen, I said, "It can't be then! That's the date of the NAPUS convention." We always had to balance family and careers.

They set their date to June 17, 1967, and we went all out to give them the best wedding we could, inviting all our family and friends, including postmaster friends of ours. Those who came from a distance were invited to stay overnight after the ceremony.

Postmasters came from Princeton, Hopkinsville, Garfield, La Grange, Crestwood and Westport. Fred Lindsey,

the NAPUS photographer, did the wedding pictures. Walter brought extra mattresses from the furniture store, and we arranged them on the floor to accommodate our pajama party. The next morning I cooked breakfast for all of us.

While the newlyweds were away on their honeymoon, I said, "Walter, will you please ask Nancy to leave gently when she takes her things?"

"How can she do that?" he asked.

"Just tell her to take a few items at a time while I'm at work. I don't want her closets all emptied at once."

No matter how she left, it was difficult for me, but we still had Rhonda at home with three more years of high school ahead. We could count on her to keep the house livened up. The newly-wed children lived in Prestonsburg, about 15 miles away, and we got to see them often. Then on June 30, 1969, their first child was born, and we were grandparents! To make that even more exciting, they named him David Walter.

As Rhonda's graduation approached and she made plans for college, we knew she needed something sturdier to drive than the Jeepster that was older than she was. After months of searching, Walter saw a pretty blue Ford Torino at Brown Motors in Paintsville and thought it would be ideal for her, but this one was brand new and a whole different deal for him. He was torn about buying her a new car. It was such a big deal to him you'd have thought he was buying the dealership.

After hours of bargaining with the dealer and wrestling with himself, he got it and Rhonda was thrilled. She had no idea how big the decision had been for him.

We helped her get settled in her dorm, and for a while she drove home on Friday evenings to spend the weekend, returning to school on Sunday.

After working all week at the post office, I looked forward to cooking Sunday dinners for the family. I spent many of my Saturdays cooking and baking and had dinner ready to serve after church on Sunday. It was a good way to enjoy family times together. Nancy's family came, and we could always count on Era and Erman to help brighten our gatherings.

One Sunday, after we'd had dinner and everybody went his or her own way, Walter decided to go to the river to fish for a while, leaving me alone. I put the food away and loaded the dishwasher, when suddenly I realized that both our girls were gone.

It didn't matter that I'd always referred to little dependable Nancy who needed instructions only once, or that Rhonda was the noisemaker who had to be reminded several times of what we wanted her to do. One was as important as the other in the makeup of our family, and now they both were gone from home. The impact of that reality hit me and I cried all afternoon.

The fact that we had so much love and happiness, and so many good times, doesn't mean that our marriage was perfect. We were young and immature when we married, but we were in love and could overlook any faults in each other. But a problem in the form of alcohol developed that was the greatest test of our marriage.

Walter was happy and congenial by nature, and he thought that sharing a drink with a friend now and then was just being likeable and fun-loving. He was unaware of any inherited weakness, but it became more difficult for him to stop drinking.

Alcohol had never been a problem in his immediate family, and I never knew either of his parents to drink at all, but Walter had two or three uncles who equated it with the water they drank and the air they breathed. He could be tolerant of his relatives and even laugh about some of their escapades, but he never meant it to happen to him.

He adored his family and never wanted to hurt us, but the problem was driving a wedge between us. It was also damaging his health and ability to enjoy life. I could write several pages about the ways it affected us, but anyone who has ever dealt with alcoholism needs no explanation, and those who have not wouldn't understand anyway.

After several unsuccessful attempts to quit drinking for the long term, Walter finally recognized that the problem was too big for him, and that's when he seriously reached out for help. He entered a private treatment facility where he spent five weeks committed to the reality that, for him, any use of alcohol was off limits.

Walter became involved in AA and was pleased to have the support of friends he made there. He had an unusual willpower, but he relied more on his Higher Power that was not just "a higher power" to him, but the Savior whose love and support were unquestionable. He earnestly sought that and it was there for him.

The organization was helpful to him and he made himself available for others who needed his help. Many mornings he was joined by an AA friend to talk and have coffee at the picnic table in our back yard. He felt it was his special mission and considered it a privilege to help others in their recovery.

He never touched alcohol again, and life was so good for all of us. He kept a motor home for travel and a houseboat for the enjoyment of family and friends, but one of our favorite fun places was our own dinner table at home. We loved having company. The grandchildren adored him and competed for the seat beside him, and mealtimes were always special when he told stories that caused us to shake with laughter.

Chapter 25

Our Special Grandchildren

Both daughters had beautiful weddings and, though it almost broke the bank, their gowns were beautiful too. In each case we just did what we knew to do and could afford. We hosted Rhonda's rehearsal dinner for 85 guests at May Lodge and even borrowed the larger Baptist church in Prestonsburg to have more room for wedding guests. We invited all our family and friends and had celebrations to remember, but this time there was no slumber party after the ceremony.

On November 14, 1972, Nancy's second son, Jonathan Lee, was born and Walter and I were settling into being grandparents. I became a little better at shopping as I loved buying little gifts for them. When David was about three, I bought the nicest little all-weather coat for him, but when he put it on, it reached the floor. He didn't grow into it for two years and the whole family gave me a hard time about that.

David called us Nanny and Pop, and the name stuck for all the others. He was only a year and a half old when we babysat one weekend before Christmas. We let him open a present and called it his Christmas party. That party grew into an annual event for him and the others as they came along and continued until the last one outgrew the custom.

He was six and Jon two when their little cousin Leigh Ann was born in 1976, and she joined them for the fun time. We always chose a Friday evening to begin so we'd have the whole weekend to celebrate. They were excited enough, but one year we sent invitations by Special Delivery mail.

Dear David, Jonathan, and Leigh Ann,

You are cordially invited to Nanny and Pop's Christmas party. It will begin after 5:00 p.m., Friday, December 15, and end Sunday afternoon. The party will begin with a spaghetti supper, served by candlelight, and dessert will be your favorite chocolate cake. Jeans will be acceptable to wear so long as they are your best ones. You should also bring your nicest pajamas as we will be taking a lot of pictures.

We will need to know if you can attend as we plan to have gifts for each one to open.

Love,
Nanny and Pop

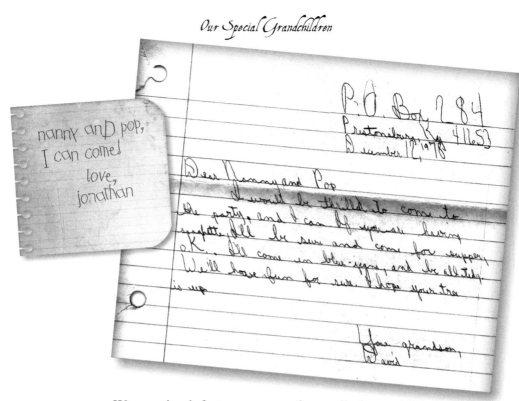

We received fast responses from all three children. Leigh Ann's mom had to help with hers but the boys drafted their own replies.

You might say the party began with the invitation, their excitement growing as they counted down the days. The boys had haircuts, and Leigh Ann got new pajamas. The fact their parents weren't invited made it even more special.

During the summer they loved being on the houseboat and were right at home on the docks where boats were parked side by side. There were always other children to play with and they loved the lake atmosphere. They enjoyed fishing, swimming or playing games on the dock and, since wearing a ski belt was a rule, we could relax about them.

When Leigh Ann was too young to even walk, we kept a child's swing on the front deck for her and she would be content for hours. She was in the open air so much that when her parents took her home, she would bawl and squall until they carried her outside. She would take a deep breath and say, "Aaaah," and we realized we had made an outdoor child of her.

Much as we loved the boat, we left it now and then to take the children for different experiences in the motor home. We usually took short trips but sometimes we took them for longer jaunts.

We left one Friday afternoon going to Natural Bridge State Park and found an RV park with a small stream nearby. Leigh Ann was just three and happy to fish with a stick with a string tied on it. We didn't risk a hook for her, but David and Jon had baited hooks and were prepared to catch the big ones.

After a ride on the sky lift the next morning, we moved on to Williamsburg and Cumberland Falls State Park where we enjoyed simple pleasures like grilling hot dogs and playing ball. As Walter drove us home Sunday evening, Leigh Ann climbed into my lap and David and Jon squeezed between us. We started telling funny stories and singing songs like *Row, row, row your boat...* We were a bunch of happy campers. Thirty-three years later, they still remember that trip.

Even before they started school, the boys were involved in sports. Jon was four when he began playing baseball in a peewee league. David also played baseball and football, but he liked tennis more and was playing competitively before he reached his teens. Leigh Ann was a grade school cheerleader, and for a time she played basketball. In one game she bumped into a player she was guarding and paused long enough to say, "Excuse me." We decided her manners might be better than her competitive spirit.

In 1979, Leigh Ann's sister Candice was born, making four grandchildren in our clan. Almost every weekend that we were home, they loved coming to what they called Pop's house. Once I wrote a poem about them that included the lines:

When night time comes they all will head
Straight for Nanny's king size bed
And as four heads lie in a row
With forty toes stuck out below...

They were easy to entertain. I took special requests for their favorite foods and after dinner, they played and romped through the house. One evening I noticed I hadn't seen Jon for a while and found him curled up in a recliner fast asleep. That night we just slipped off his shoes and pants, but we came up with a plan. When telling the others to wash their hands for dinner, we would tell Jon to get into his pajamas.

Once I noticed David was in the bathroom a good while and went to check. He said, "Nanny, I finally got this off the wall." I had spent days finding a tissue holder that would stick to the tile without screws.

One night they started clamoring for me to read them a story, and I said, "I can't. I don't have my glasses." They were persistent so I reached for a book and improvised on the story of *The Three Bears.* I said, "Mama Bear cooked soup beans and they all got gas and had to go walking in the woods." Soon they were giggling and taking in every word. After that they often asked, "Nanny, read us a story without your glasses."

When little Kelly Marie came along in 1984, she turned out to be the only shy one. She would peek around her mother's skirt tail, too bashful to talk. To celebrate her fifth birthday, the family vacationed in Disney World where Rhonda arranged a special birthday surprise at the Hoop Dee Doo Review. Everything went according to plan but, when Kelly was invited on stage, she crawled under the table and wouldn't come out.

Our grandchildren have been so special, and we enjoyed them all. We hoped that, after they were grown and gone, they would remember the special times we planned for them. The happiness we provided them was returned to us many times over, and the frolics we shared are recorded in our memory books forever.

Our Special Grandchildren

Along with the children born into our family, there have been others so dear that I would be proud to claim them as my own. Wayne Chewning didn't have to be kin to steal my heart away with his bright smile and his zest for living. It's been years since he was taken from us in the prime of his life, leaving a great void and a reminder that life is very fragile. I never stopped missing him.

Another is Gwen Clark Tackett, a very special lady who calls me her other mother. Our families share a warm regard and we'd swim the river for each other – if we could swim at all.

And Phillip Fields is a young man who has spent the last nine years serving our country aboard ship in the U. S. Navy. I started sending him notes and care packages the first time he was deployed, and he uses a cell phone and e-mail to contact me from around the world. I call him my other grandson, and he calls me Nanny, just as the other grandchildren do. I might need to swim the ocean for him – and he knows I would try if he asked.

Chapter 26
Postal Career

I soon regretted any reluctance I'd ever felt about being a postmaster for I was truly in my element on the job. I loved my customers and along with giving them good service, I was determined to make their contacts with the office an enjoyable experience. We provided their postal needs with a smile, chatted with them and showed concern for their well being. It was obvious that most of them looked forward to coming in.

I told my clerks it was the same price to enjoy the work, and I'll always believe we accomplished more by maintaining a pleasant atmosphere. That's quite a contrast to the work in later years when stress became so pronounced that a new phrase was coined about "going postal." It was a sad indictment against the profession I loved.

I will always be glad that my career spanned a time when, though pay was minimal, service was the major concern. The sense of achievement was its own reward, and the goodwill I've enjoyed is priceless.

After being elected state secretary for NAPUS, I was invited to a dinner in Cincinnati to honor the retirement of the regional director.

For that dinner, I sat across the table from Loren Gard. We were all sharing information about our different offices and the challenges we dealt with. Someone told about having antiquated equipment, and I told about my desk that had been in a flood and no amount of scrubbing would get all the mud out of the drawers. I saw Mr. Gard take a note pad from his pocket and scribble something.

Back at work, I had a call from him saying, "I've just checked on some surplus equipment we have. There's a solid oak desk that needs a little refinishing, but it doesn't have any mud in it. Do you think you could use it?"

Could I use it? I would love it! It had been an executive's desk and I enjoyed using it for the next 24 years. Almost every postal inspector or manager at any level who came by my office asked, "Where did you get that desk?" Sometime after I retired, I noticed the desk was gone. Wherever it is, I know it has my fingerprints all over it.

Serving as secretary meant attending any meeting of postmasters, whether county, district, state or national. It involved making speeches and writing articles for postal publications, and sometimes it meant serving as go-between for postmasters and their managers.

Many times I went to the managers with a cause for some NAPUS member. In each situation, the parties came to understand each other a little better.

When I first went to Betsy Layne, the office had two hours per day of clerk time. This worked well for a while, but every day became a little busier. I was surprised one afternoon to get a call from a regional official who said, "Some of us have talked about your situation, and we think you could use some extra clerk time." I've never heard of another postmaster being told that, as almost every office could use more clerk hours. My caller continued, "So much of what you do helps the Post Office Department as much as it helps the National Association, and we want you to have the time you need." They tripled my weekly clerk time.

No postmaster reading this will ever believe I got an increase in clerk time. They even let me hire a second part-time clerk to assure the office would be covered when I traveled, and Ganell Clark became an important part of our work.

The Justell post office was closed and made a branch of our office. It was run by an officer-in-charge who reported daily business transactions to us. We had to do periodic audits of the station, just as the postal inspectors did of our main office. They only checked us about once a year, but their visits were always unannounced.

During my early years on the job, the nation was divided into fifteen regions with a director for each one. Ours was in Cincinnati. In 1970, the Post Office Department became the U. S. Postal Service and the whole system was realigned. Now there were five regions, and while a Postmaster General still headed the whole thing, we would also have five Regional PMGs.

Our regional headquarters was in Chicago. The chain of command was broken down further into districts and sectional center facilities, and each of these had a manager. For many years, my SCF Manager was the Hazard Postmaster, and we had a great working relationship.

Sometimes he asked me to write for the bulletin he issued to the four counties he supervised, and once he requested an article about postmasters' personal appearance. I said, "Mr. Tayloe, surely we all try to look as good as we can." But he said, "No, in some offices I go to, postmasters have failed to comb their hair, put their teeth in, clean their shoes and such as that." I never knew who had disappointed him, but he took his duties seriously.

I wrote the article, but didn't mention these specific things. I wrote: *When we open our door for business we never know who our customers might be. It could even be the Governor or the President, so we should be ready to greet them, and our appearance should reflect our respect for any customer.*

I thought it was a one-time thing when I was asked to train a new area postmaster. My first such assignment was in an office smaller than mine, but soon there were others and the distances became farther out. One assignment was in Greenup, and I reminded my supervisor that since the office was larger than mine I wasn't familiar with all the procedures. He said my grasp of basics was enough and they'd have someone else cover whatever areas I suggested. I was their trainer of choice for all but the largest offices. For fourteen years, whenever a new postmaster was appointed within my range, I could expect a call from whomever my manager was at the time.

Whatever expectations I had about travel were like a drop in the bucket. During five years as state secretary and one year as state president, there were so many places to go. If not a regularly scheduled meeting, it would be to represent the organization at some occasion or to honor some person. If it were a national figure being recognized, I represented the state. These functions were important in the overall picture and in being a good officer.

I could never have done it had Walter not been supportive. Whenever I mentioned a trip, he'd say something like, "I guess you need your car serviced," but he never made a remark like, "Not again!" He knew I had a job to do, and he liked the same consideration when he had a business trip – and especially for a fishing trip.

For a time, we had Jackie Strange as manager of the Kentuckiana District (Kentucky and part of Indiana). Her office and home were in Louisville, and one day she called and asked me to come visit her. She knew I wrote for both the state and national publications of NAPUS, and she had an assignment for me. She was initiating a new procedure for mail handling that would be used first in the New Albany, Indiana, Post Office. She wanted me to observe and write about the program and explain it to other postal managers. She cooked dinner for us when I arrived on Sunday evening. We both spent the following day in the New Albany office. My article ran in *Postmasters Gazette*, and she was pleased with it.

She soon contacted me again with a request that I participate in a nationwide work criteria study. I never knew who the other writers were, but Ms. Strange trusted me with assignments, and our friendship continued, even after she became Deputy Postmaster General.

I loved the everyday routine of running my office and the one-on-one contacts with the many personalities of my customers. Some had a funny story each time they came. Some thanked us profusely for the good service, and others complained no matter how hard we tried to please them. Once in a while someone cried on my shoulder about some circumstance I could only help by listening, but it was obvious they trusted me. It was a compliment and an honor I never took for granted.

I enjoyed most of the special assignments, especially one to cover a first day of issue of a stamp honoring Jackie Robinson, the first black baseball player to play in the Major Leagues. Governor A. B. "Happy" Chandler was the key figure in that program held at his famous cabin in Versailles. There was a whole list of special guests, including my old friend Inspector Gene Pinson and a few former baseball players. Governor Chandler was the Commissioner of Baseball who made the historic decision allowing Robinson to play. I was to write the story for postal publications.

I arrived early for the program, and Governor and Mrs. Chandler gave me a tour of the two-story cabin, telling me of the many guests who had occupied its rooms. He called her "Mama Chandler," and they just beamed when they looked at each other. He had a wonderful memory, and whenever I saw him again, he'd always mention that visit.

My most challenging assignment was arranged by regional and district headquarters. I was asked to oversee the making of a video depicting how the postal service reaches into rural America.

The finished product would be used as a training film across the nation. I would be assisted by Barbara Brand,

Postmaster of Jeffersonville, and a film crew. The project required spending several days at the headquarters office in Chicago to learn what our managers wanted and to plan the shooting schedule.

We met the three-man crew in Lexington on Sunday evening. Early Monday, we were at the airport to meet an incoming mail plane. We filmed the landing and transport of mail to the post office on Nandino Boulevard, and to the offices of the VA Center on Leestown Road.

From Lexington, we went to Montgomery County, where we filmed rural settings. Barbara didn't join us when the crew came to my area on Monday, but we went right to work filming our mountainous terrain and the different enterprises here. We learned what time a train would be pulling 100 cars of coal out of Johns Creek and set up on a hill to catch the impressive scene. We also went to a coal processing plant at Ivel to show how coal was washed and graded, and then to the company's offices to show how the Postal Service fit into their operation.

We followed a rural carrier as she traveled our winding roads, across bridges and beautiful streams. We even found a swinging bridge, one of the last in our area, and showed the carrier crossing it. We went to small businesses and private homes, quaint shops and ball parks, anything at all to depict "Rural America" being served by the U. S. Mail.

We had the *Postal Manual* as our guidebook, and every week we received the Postal Bulletin to announce any changes in policy or regulations. There were always safety reminders, but no warning could safeguard every situation.

One afternoon I'd gone into the storage room to fold empty mail sacks and to straighten up items stored on the

Postal Career

metal shelving. I was absorbed in the work when the telephone started ringing with a strange and urgent sound. Ganell had customers at the window, so I stopped what I was doing to take the call. I picked up the phone and heard a dial tone – there was no one on the line. With the phone still in my hand, I heard a crash that shook our whole building. Ganell and I both ran to see what had happened.

A heavy refrigeration truck, parked on an incline behind our building, had lost its brakes and came rolling downhill. The impact caused the sharp top of the metal door to slam against the steel shelving where I had stood just a few seconds earlier. Had I not moved, it would have cut me in two.

There was no one on the line when I answered – but guardian angels can do their work without talking at all. The call was meant for me.

Truck Runs Wild, Rams Postoffice

A runaway ice truck crashed halfway through the Betsy Layne postoffice building last Thursday morning, missing the postmistress, Aileen Hall, and a Postal Service clerk, Ganell Clark, by only a few feet. Mrs. Hall estimated the damage to be "at least $2000."

The report of the incident said the driver of the truck had parked on the grade at the Texaco gasoline station, across the old highway from the postoffice, and had placed a rock beneath a tire to hold it. When he started the motor for the freezer generator of the truck, the vehicle began rolling.

The truck penetrated the section of the building which is used for storage of incoming and outgoing mail. It hit a door, buckling the steel door-frame, crumpled the wall and practically demolished a storage cabinet. The truck also damaged the bumper and fender of Mrs. Hall's auto.

It was the second "motorized invasion" of the postoffice. Earlier, an auto rammed into the rear of the building.

Chapter 27
National Conventions

It's fortunate that I always loved working – at almost anything except washing dishes and ironing clothes. I didn't have to do either at the post office. And if I loved my job, my work in our national association was like icing on the cake.

Meetings and conventions are necessary in any organization and they require a lot of work, but there can also be fringe benefits. In my case, they allowed me to go places I never expected and to work with people I admired. I worked on committees with people from our largest cities and there was no distinction in the size of our office. It was our willingness to work that mattered.

My first national convention was in Omaha, Nebraska in 1965. I flew out of Lexington and was over Indianapolis when the pilot's voice came over the intercom, "Ladies and gentlemen, we're experiencing engine problems and have to turn back." I looked to see the reactions of the other passengers who may have been churning inside, but they appeared calm. I didn't recognize the angels on board, but one could have been my seatmate and I wouldn't have known.

Just seconds later, the same voice said, "You may see a black streak go by your window but don't be alarmed. We're dumping fuel and want you to know what it is." No sooner had he said it than a black "swoosh" started by my window. I hadn't flown a lot and never alone, but I kept my composure.

When we approached Cincinnati, the nearest airport, emergency vehicles were spaced up and down the runway with emergency lights flashing. They had sprayed the runway with flame-retardant foam and sat waiting for the landing. We deplaned quickly and without trouble but I would have gone home right then if I could.

The emergency caused a long delay and I arrived in Omaha at 3:00 a.m., weary and worn. States were usually grouped together in the hotels so I was surrounded by other Kentuckians who looked after me at my first national. The postmasters I met were just like our Kentucky bunch – easy to know, easy to like. A group of us were walking together toward the convention center when I shot out ahead of them all. I heard someone say, "Watch that farmer go!" I told them I once had to walk a mile just to catch the school bus and they thought I was joking.

My second national was hosted by my own state in Louisville. Postmaster Bremer Ehrler got right to work with a planning committee. Hosting from three to four thousand guests for five days meant a lot of work. Word got around that I was willing to work and he named me to the special guest committee. We were responsible for meeting official guests upon arrival and seeing that they received a proper welcome.

National Conventions

In 1968, convention was in Washington, DC, and it was one of the most exciting ever. President Lyndon Johnson addressed one of the first sessions and welcomed us to the city.

The huge Washington Hilton Hotel was headquarters for the meeting, and my room was across the hall from Bobbie Hunter of Providence, Kentucky. Soon we were eating and walking to the convention hall together. She had been Secretary to President Johnson when he was a Texas Senator. When he became a candidate for Vice President, she traveled with him and Lady Bird during the campaign. They had expected her to stay on in DC after he was elected but she wanted to go home to Kentucky. When asked what she would like most to do, she said, "I'd like to be the postmaster for my hometown of Providence." That wasn't hard for him to work out, and their ties weren't severed when he became President.

Besides being fun to be around, Bobbie knew points of interest in Washington. One evening we got a cab to drive us

over the city and she was a wonderful tour guide. She pointed out a window at a Senate office building and said, "That was my office." I wondered how she could give up a career like that, but I know there are times when we all want to go home.

Bobbie made a call to Liz Carpenter, the First Lady's press secretary, and asked if she might bring a few guests to the White House for a visit. Ms. Carpenter assured her she would be most welcome. She would need a list of Bobbie's guests in advance, and I was delighted to be one of twenty invited to go.

We were met by Ms. Carpenter who took us through the kitchen and into the china room for a brief wait before going on to a corridor outside the President's office. There we were met Mrs. Johnson who shook our hand, calling each by name as Bobbie introduced us. She invited us to attend a special ceremony, then excused herself to go join her husband.

The President's Social Secretary, Bess Abell, was there to escort us outside to witness the ceremony. We stood with a small group beneath a balcony to watch the President's official welcome to a visiting ambassador from the African country of Chad.

We enjoyed watching the helicopter land on the south lawn where a limousine awaited to bring the visiting party up the circular drive. We watched our President and First Lady greet the ambassador as he stepped out on the red carpet. We were close enough to hear their exchange, followed by a 21 gun salute and music by the Marine Band. Secret Service agents scanned our group all the while and, when the ceremony ended, we saw we were standing near Luci Johnson Nugent and her small son.

National Conventions

Bess Clements Abell, daughter of Senator Earle Clements, was Bobbie's friend from western Kentucky. Her husband, Tyler Abell, was being installed the next day as Chief of Protocol in a ceremony at the State Department. Bess invited Bobbie to that, and this time she took only two friends, Jim Syers and me.

The guest list for that ceremony was impressive and included Jack Anderson, the famous columnist and close associate of Drew Pearson, but I especially enjoyed getting to visit with Senator Clements. He'd been both Governor and Senator of Kentucky, but preferred the latter title. In making conversation with him I said, "Senator, It must be nice to have so many friends." He corrected me. "No, I have many acquaintances – and a few friends." He expanded some on that comment, and I later wrote a column for Postmasters Gazette about that visit.

In 1969, we went to Hot Springs, Arkansas. I drove to Providence and stayed overnight with Bobbie and we went on together. One highlight of that meeting was electing fellow Kentuckian Bremer Ehrler as National President. Also, recognition was given at conventions for work we had done through the year, and I received the first of three first-place awards for articles I had written for our state paper. During the five years I served as state secretary, we won four first place awards for our work in membership.

Ehrler was the presiding officer for the next two conventions – Philadelphia, Pennsylvania, in 1970, and Anaheim, California, in 1971, where they closed Disneyland to the public one evening to give our delegates complete enjoyment of the park.

The following year, we met in Salt Lake City, Utah. It was 1972, the year I was president of our state chapter, and I was asked to do a nominating speech for John Goodman of Illinois to be National Secretary/Treasurer. As I looked out at that huge audience I thought of the little speech I had to give as a junior in high school when I wished the floor would swallow me. Speeches never came easy for me, but I learned to grit my teeth and do them. Salt Lake City was also where I got to observe some Mormon history, visit the famous Beehive House and attend a televised performance of the Mormon Tabernacle Choir. A small group of us went out to Park City to visit a retired friend, and for a long time after, her elderly parents sent messages to the "little postmaster from Kentucky."

We met in 1973 at a huge Jewish resort in Lake Kiamesha, New York. It had a distinctive atmosphere and delicious food, different from anything we had anywhere else. Convention was in Seattle the following year, where we enjoyed a salmon barbecue on Puget Sound and dinner at the famous Space Needle Restaurant.

In 1975, convention was in Miami, Florida, and the following year, Minneapolis, Minnesota. The latter was made memorable by an address by former Vice President and Senator Hubert H. Humphrey who touched us with one of the most inspiring messages I ever heard. The doors to convention hall were closed, and no one left or entered as he held an audience of four thousand postmasters spellbound. I was thrilled to be in that audience.

I served on the special guest committee at that meeting and went with John Miller to meet a well known Wyoming

Senator at the airport. We took him to the hotel and, as he registered, he said to the clerk, "By the way, I like fresh strawberries for breakfast."

"Sir, you're in Minnesota, and strawberries are not in season."

"Then have some flown in," he ordered.

I never did check to see if he got his berries, but he'd fallen from grace a little in my eyes. It was interesting to see traits of some pretty important people. Many were genuinely fine, and some were a little carried away with themselves.

When we went to Phoenix the following year, my neighboring postmaster, Jack Stumbo, was on the special guest committee. He and a postmaster from California were asked to pick up her congressman at the airport. Since my flight was due in at the same time, Jack said they would pick me up too. While she met her guest at one gate, he met me at another. The airlines had lost my luggage and we were delayed a bit for them to get a description of it. As we rode back to the hotel, I asked the congressman if he knew our Carl Perkins. "Of course I know him," he replied. "He walks up and down the halls of Congress in those white socks and big feet." Jack and I decided he was arrogant.

We checked into the hotel side by side, and he asked the clerk, "Is there a refrigerator in my room?"

"No, Sir," was the reply.

"Then have one put in," he demanded.

Jack took him to the hospitality room and someone asked, "Where have you been? We've been expecting you."

"Well," he said, "some gal from Kentucky lost her luggage and we had to wait at the airport."

Jack and I giggled to ourselves about it, and we didn't care a lot that he was unhappy. He surely had no concern about my luggage.

The next year, a group of us drove to St. Louis and, while there, I defied my claustrophobia and went up in that famous arch. I also got to see some hot-air balloons lift off. Again, I did a nominating speech, this time for another Kentucky Postmaster, Jim Syers of Sturgis. He was the second postmaster from our state to be elected National President.

When we arrived in Los Angeles in 1980, there was a message waiting from my brother David, now retired and living in South Lake Tahoe. His grandson had been killed by a drunk driver in Sacramento. Services were postponed by investigations, and he asked me not to come right away. I confided to only two best friends, Jean and Delma, what happened as I couldn't talk about it and stay there. When the meeting ended, my daughter Rhonda and granddaughter Leigh Ann flew out to meet me for the service and to spend a few days with this beloved brother.

In 1981, Walter went with me and drove his motor home to convention in Oklahoma City. Jim and Clarice Chambers of Westport traveled with us and on to California for another visit with David. I was surprised at the Oklahoma convention to be one of six people called to the podium to receive a special award by the Air Transport Association of America called The Order of The Vest.

In 1982 we met in Biloxi, Mississippi, and when convention ended, we went on to New Orleans for some sightseeing and a cruise on the Delta Queen. The next year we went to San Juan, Puerto Rico, and Delma Smith and I shared a room at the Dupont Plaza Hotel that connected to one with John and Elsie Miller of Lexington. John was much like a brother to me, but he was dying of cancer and we treasured the time with them. I made another nominating speech in San Juan, this time for Jim  Copham of McDonald, Ohio, to be National President.

The 1984 convention in Columbus, Ohio has a chapter all it's own, but we met in Las Vegas in 1985. Our beloved John Miller had lost his valiant battle with cancer and I did a eulogy for him. He was one of the most well-known and respected members of our organization.

I retired March 31, 1986, but still attended the convention in San Antonio, Texas, where I enjoyed a boat ride by the River Walk and visited the Alamo. I missed the next one in Portland, Oregon, but in 1988, Elfreda Bowen and I drove to Virginia Beach, Virginia, through beautiful country while fall colors were at their peak.

I was doing a regular column for Postmasters Gazette called Off The Clock in 1989, so when time came, I flew to San Francisco for my third California convention. Rhonda and her friend Kitty went along, and they rented a car to explore the area while I enjoyed convention.

In 1991, granddaughter Leigh Ann and I went to Honolulu, Hawaii. Our room had a beautiful view overlooking Waikiki Beach. We took a tour of the island, saw several shows and visited Pearl Harbor, Diamond Head Crater, Punch Bowl Cemetery and other points of interest.

The following year, I went with good friend Jean Hall and her sister Margaret to convention in Nashville, Tennessee. We stayed at Opryland Hotel, and attended the Grand Old Opry one evening. Then in 1998, Delma Smith and I flew to Fort Lauderdale, Florida, for convention and another great time together.

My career was a gift I had no way of foreseeing. It allowed me to have so many friends all across the country. We worked together for the good of our profession and our country, and I've never known a more service-minded or patriotic group of people than the postmasters of my time.

Chapter 28
The Campaign

Once again we were in Washington, DC, for the National Legislative Conference scheduled each year in February. The agenda included business sessions and dinners but the part I enjoyed most was visiting our respective legislators. We had seven Congressmen and two Senators who welcomed us to their offices and sometimes joined us for dinner.

The year was 1984 and on our first day there I was approached by a delegation from several states. They wanted to know if I'd be a candidate for the office of National Secretary/Treasurer. I'd never even considered such a thing, and the idea sounded absurd. "I have no desire to do that," I said, "and besides it's too late to jump into a race. The election is in August and the president endorsed a candidate a long time ago. They've campaigned for more than a year."

"But he can be beat," they insisted, "and you're the one to do it. We'll help organize a campaign. Just tell us you'll run."

The Campaign

I kept giving them reasons for not running, and they countered each one. Finally, I said, "Walter Hall would kill me if I even mentioned such a thing." Most of them, especially the Kentucky bunch, knew Walter well and doubted he would do that.

Jim Chambers said, "How about calling him to see what he thinks?" The room was nearly full when I dialed our number and said, "Walter, a group of these people are urging me to run for national office, and I'm telling them I can't do such a thing."

I knew they would accept thumbs down from him, but his response was, "Why not?"

The television monitors in the lobby of the Capitol Hilton ran an announcement all the next day:

Reception for Aileen Hall
Candidate for National Secretary/Treasurer
Suite 802, 6:00 p.m.

That was the beginning of the whirlwind I would be in for the next six months.

The reception suite was set up for guests to come in one door and go out another, and the room was always full. People didn't just shake my hand, they hugged me and pledged support. Someone later said we had counted 500 guests, close to the number attending the conference.

Walter wrote the first check to start a campaign fund, and soon other contributions were coming in. We got organized with a campaign chairman and treasurer and a list of

The Campaign

committees. Supporters quilted blankets, crocheted items, framed prints and contributed other things to be raffled or sold at auction. More than $100,000 went into the special checking account. That sounds like a lot of money, but many supporters helped campaign and travel was expensive.

Walter went with me on my first campaign visit to Columbus, Ohio, where we attended the state officers' meeting. As we prepared to leave, we found our car had been vandalized. The passenger window was broken and two hubcaps were missing. The hotel helped us get the window replaced, but with two hubcaps missing, our car appeared to be limping down the road.

Our daughter Rhonda was just starting her advertising agency, and one of her first projects was to design and produce banners, posters and brochures for the campaign. We had these along with pins and stickers that read: "All for Hall in '84."

NAPUS politics is serious business to the membership, so we go all out in our convictions. I loved believing in a candidate and supporting him or her. During my career we elected three Kentuckians to the office of National President, and it was exciting to be a part of that. We were honest and open with each other but, before this election was over, I would see a tougher side of politics.

It wasn't possible to visit every convention in

six months. I might have made more but some states chose the same dates. In those cases, we tried to attend smaller gatherings such as the Spring Fling near Summersville, West Virginia. Sometimes we even backtracked. Once, we went to Oklahoma City for a meeting, and a month later we passed our same hotel on our way to New Mexico.

There were many experiences I'll always remember, some funny. At one state convention, the president told me I had five minutes to speak. I was almost through telling them why they should choose me when a little bell rang and she said, "Time's up!" I was mid-sentence and she cut me off with four words left. It wasn't that she didn't like me – I received their unanimous endorsement.

One long trip was in Walter's motor home to Springfield, Massachusetts, where they had a gathering called the New England Council, made up of that state, Maine, Rhode Island, New Hampshire, Connecticut, and Vermont. Jim and Clarice Chambers and Delma Smith went with us. We knew the president was popular there and they would honor his endorsement, but we went and mingled and saw many old friends. It was one of only two meetings my opponent and I both attended.

The most exciting convention for me was in Chicago. Four fellow Kentuckians and two postmasters from Ohio went along to campaign for me. Illinois was supposed to make an endorsement on Tuesday, so we planned to check out that evening. Then someone had the vote changed to Wednesday. When I asked to hold the room Jean and I shared, they said it wasn't available. They extended reservations for my Ohio friends but hadn't connected them with my campaign. It was only my room they wanted.

The Campaign

Our group huddled to make a decision. There were other hotels close, but I needed to be there, right in the midst. I went to the front desk again to persuade the clerk to let me keep my room, but she repeated that she was sorry, they had to have it. One of our Ohio friends "just happened" to be in the lobby, and he stepped over to ask, "Is it only her room you need?"

"Yes."

"Then she can have ours." As our friends were gathering up their luggage to move across the street, they got a call from the front desk saying they wouldn't have to move after all because someone had canceled. They moved anyway.

During the morning business session, the president announced they had 300 members present and each would get a ballot. We were seated at tables for ten, and I reminded our group that it would take 151 to win. We knew it was close and were really tense as we waited. When it was over, someone announced, "Hall, 158." I squealed, "We got it!" Winning the whole election could have been no more exciting.

We came home elated but preparing to travel again, this time to Corinth, Mississippi. I laundered some clothes and my friend Thelma did my hair.

The Mississippi bunch was in my corner from the beginning. I stayed positive and never mentioned my opponent. I always started my speech with some humor, and when they laughed, I relaxed. I told about my record of service in my state and national assignments. Then when I asked for their support, I usually got it.

I had access to Kentucky Colonel commissions arranged by the Secretary of State. We commissioned about 150 people across the country as Kentucky Colonels.

The Campaign

I was granted a spot on the program in every state I visited and was sometimes in pretty elite company. In North Carolina, I followed Governor James Hunt, Jr., and in Texas, Senator Phil Gramm followed me. In South Carolina, I followed Postmaster General William Bolger. Usually, the PMG is ushered in to give his address, then ushered out again, but this time, Mr. Bolger sat down and listened to my spiel.

While Walter never liked attending my regular meetings, he loved the campaign. The Georgia convention was in Savannah and he wanted to go where we had honeymooned thirty-eight years earlier. This time I would steer clear of the surf. With his personality he was a great help in meeting people, and he felt right at home with those Georgia friends. They didn't seem to be aware that I had an opponent for I had their full support. By way of a social time, they had a watermelon slicing that was like a picnic. It was a fun way to meet members while we ate and talked and spit seeds on the ground.

I was home only long enough to get ready again, this time for Minnesota. I flew into the twin cities of Minneapolis/St. Paul, and some of our Kentucky group drove up to help campaign. My chairman there was concerned about support and asked that the vote be split. It was a bad call for we got 63% when we could have had the total vote.

Some of our trips were long and a little hazardous. Walter and two fellow postmasters, Mike Bourne and David

The Campaign

Games, went with me to Oklahoma City. On our return, we stopped for the night and ate at a truck stop. The next morning the guys had to carry me to the car and all three rode up front so I could lie down in the back seat. When we stopped for them to eat lunch, they practically carried me to the ladies' room. After a bit, Walter sent a lady to check on me and she found me lying on the floor.

They took me to a doctor who diagnosed severe food poisoning. He said it had been in my system way too long and I was fortunate to have survived. I told him Someone was watching over me.

I barely had time to recuperate before Walter and I drove to Albuquerque, New Mexico. We had a lot of fun at their masquerade party, and I was surprised by the support they gave me.

One of my most extensive campaign trips took eight full days. My first destination was San Antonio where I was met by a few Texas friends. After two days there, I had their endorsement and headed out to Spokane, Washington. Fellow Kentuckian R. C. Day flew out to help campaign. R. C.'s cousin Bill was a postmaster there, and Bill and his wife Terri hosted a "Meet the Candidate" reception. They prepared all the food and brought it from home. Gestures such as that continue to warm my heart.

My opponent was in Spokane, the one state convention we both attended. I won their endorsement before going on to Spearfish, South Dakota.

The Campaign

Postmaster Marion Pulliam was serving double airport duty. He brought our soon to be PMG Paul Carlin, for a flight back to Washington while picking me up for the drive to Spearfish. On the way to his boarding gate, Mr. Carlin and I spotted each other and he stepped across the heavy rope to wish me well. Afterwards, Marion gave me a tour of his Rapid City office. He had been the postmaster at Bardstown, Kentucky, and it was a little like having family meet me.

While in Spearfish, a postmaster we called "Chief" and his wife drove me through Spearfish Canyon, and I loved that. We had lunch at an old saloon that had a chair mounted over the door, the one Wild Bill Hickok was sitting in when he was shot and killed.

I left that convention during their final business session to start my journey home. We took a detour by Mt. Rushmore, passing a herd of wild buffalo along the way.

When we went to the Missouri convention, it was becoming apparent that I could win. Their membership embraced me and assured me I would have their vote. It was customary for NAPUS to assign one top national officer to

The Campaign

each state convention, but the day before the Missouri vote, the president himself came and brought the entire top staff. They set up a hospitality room and invited members to meet the president. My opponent didn't attend, but when the votes were cast next day, he had their endorsement.

My own state convention came soon after the disappointing outcome in Missouri, and I told our group we were wasting time and money, and I wanted to drop out.

They were adamant that we go on and even enlisted Walter's help to change my mind. They would keep raising money and would rather lose than quit. So the whirlwind continued.

Walter, Jim Chambers and I drove to Bettendorff, Iowa, on a Sunday, and our hosts took us on a river boat cruise that evening. I spoke at their business session the next morning and was pleased to get their endorsement before heading out to a barbeque that evening in Manhattan, Kansas.

When we arrived, the barbecue was already under way. President Sweitzer told the band to take a break and he gave me the microphone. I stood between musical instruments and electrical equipment to give my speech and we left Kansas with another endorsement.

We drove all night to get to Fayetteville, Arkansas, with Walter and Jim taking turns at the wheel. We enjoyed the two days we spent there but the state endorsed my opponent.

Our last state convention was in Lafayette, Louisiana, where we really needed their endorsement to win. On our first evening, the hosts had a crayfish boil. I'd never eaten crayfish, and wasn't sure I wanted to, but it was a delicacy to them and I decided I should try it. I did pass on the alligator I was offered the next night.

We loved Louisiana and they obviously loved us. I was their candidate and their support was understood. Then the NAPUS staff came the evening before the vote. My opponent didn't attend at all but when the votes were counted, he had their endorsement.

When that convention ended, New Orleans Postmaster Jim Gard expressed disdain about what had happened. I said, "Believe me, it's all right if we lose. You see how strongly this president opposes me, and he still has another year in office. It would be very difficult to work with him now."

I thought about the World's Fair going on in New Orleans and said, "I wish we'd arranged to stop at the fair but it's too late now." Jim said, "Maybe not," and walked away.

Soon he returned with a phone number. "You have a room at the Hyatt. When you walk out of the hotel, you can go directly into the fairgrounds. They're waiting for you to call to say how long you can stay."

We had a beautiful room and spent two full days enjoying the fair and finding little gifts for the grandchildren. It was a good way for the whirlwind to wind down.

A few states withheld their votes until the national convention, but I couldn't count on them. I knew from the beginning we didn't have enough time, and yet the membership enjoyed a good race. Not one person ever complained that we could have done more or that it took too much effort. Everyone who participated seemed to have had a good time. Certainly I did.

As we headed home, we were at peace knowing we had given the race our best shot. We talked about interesting events from the past weeks and some of the wonderful people who had carved their names on our hearts.

Chapter 29
Concession Speech

After the Louisiana convention I knew I should start working on a concession speech. I called my good friend Jim Copham in Ohio to ask if he would critique my first draft. After reading it he called to say, "I wouldn't change a word, but I have to tell you, you won't be able to deliver it."

"What do you mean?" I asked. He said, "When you get to the part about your family and fellow postmasters, it will be too emotional for you so you'd better re-word it some way."

National convention was held in Columbus, Ohio, and on the day for election of officers, the procedure took some time. There were nominating speeches for both candidates, then the complete roll call of states. When the votes were tabulated, he had ten percent more than I.

When all that was completed, the president resumed the program without offering either of us time to thank our supporters. After all that work, money spent and miles

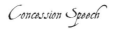

traveled, and after writing and rewriting my concession speech, I wouldn't be allowed to give it. But the campaign committee wouldn't give up, and Jim Chambers said to me, "Don't you leave this hall for anything. Just stay ready."

Whether or not angels involve themselves in such matters, I have no idea, but just then an urgent call came for the president, leaving the secretary in charge of the podium. Jim saw his chance and insisted that I be allowed to thank my supporters. The Secretary conceded, "She can have two minutes and that's all." I was there before he could change his mind.

I had gone through the emotion of the words as I wrote them and had that out of the way. I wanted to prove Copham wrong about not being able to do it so I concentrated on the delivery. There was some cheering from supporters when I stepped to the podium, giving me a minute to look at the audience of more than 3,000. Judy from Illinois sat on the front row with tears rolling down her face, and I made a mental note not to look at her again.

I was aware of the two minute time limit but saw the crowd was "with me," and I knew the platform was mine until I relinquished it. They wouldn't dare cut me short with that many people interested. I looked at Walter sitting on the edge of his seat. He winked and nodded as if to say, "You can do it!" and it made me smile. Then I began.

"Fellow Postmasters and Friends,

"I can relate to the old guy who was arrested and hailed into court, charged with intoxication and setting fire to his hotel bed. He said, 'Your Honor, I'll admit to having a little sip, but I want you to know that bed was on fire when I got in it!' Truly, this campaign was fired up before I even got near it.

Concession Speech

"This is my 20th national convention, and a funny thing happened on the way this time. I got caught up in a campaign that has been one of the most interesting, most rewarding experiences of my life. The tellers verify that we have 2,718 votes possible, and I received 45% of those. I am pleased, even thrilled, to have had such support in a campaign that lasted only six months.

"It was not possible to get to every state, but we did travel to the four corners of the nation – 30,000 by auto and another 25,000 by plane. I drove by the arch in St. Louis four times and flew over it twice. In one week of travel, I went through airports in Lexington, Atlanta, San Antonio, Denver (3 times), Spokane, Rapid City, and Chicago. This allowed me to attend three state conventions – Texas, Washington and South Dakota.

"In some long journeys, we made only one or two states, but we accomplished much of what we set out to do. We gave postmasters a choice. This office is worth having to work for.

"We hear comments from the membership now and then that people want to be on the winning side. If this is your main concern, then I apologize to the states that endorsed me. But unless I learn that you regret your support, this campaign is far from a failure.

"People who fail are those who have aspirations they are capable of but they lack the courage to try. We had the courage to try, and we have the grace to accept your decision.

"When I say this has been one of the most rewarding experiences of my life, it's because it taught me some things I didn't know. I knew my fellow postmasters – from all states – were great, but some of you have overwhelmed me with your kindness, your warmth and your generosity. To elaborate on these would be too emotional for me, but you have my promise that I'll always love you.

"There's a bunch of you from Kentucky that I have worked alongside for all these years. I thought I knew you well. You have worked to raise funds, written letters, made phone calls, shared the miles traveled, shared the meals, the victories and the disappointments. You're much more dear than I knew, and I'll never be able to thank you enough.

"I even learned my own family better. Our daughters – Rhonda who designed my brochures, banners and posters; Nancy who kept track of our travels and progress from her home in Florida; and the grandchildren who enjoyed all those tee shirts we brought from so many states.

"And finally Walter, who amazed me with his support and encouragement, who totally missed his favorite fishing season to run all across the country with me. He has indulged me many things in our years together, but his help in this effort has been the very ultimate. Together, we have loved the special people and the special places we visited. It's an experience I wouldn't have missed for all the world.

"I once read a quote about Success by Ralph Waldo Emerson that I liked and have altered slightly:

> *It is to laugh often and love much,*
> *To win the respect of intelligent persons;*
> *To earn the approval of honest critics,*
> *And to appreciate beauty wherever it is found.*
> *It is to give of one's self,*
> *To have accomplished a task,*
> *And to feel you have made some contribution*
> *To your little corner of the world.*

Concession Speech

"A couple of years ago, my District Manager asked me to attend a program and do a story on a statesman who, among other things, is a former United States Senator and former Governor of Kentucky – A. B. "Happy" Chandler. Gov. Chandler made some profound remarks that day, and one of them expresses best my feelings now: 'We always hoped we might win the respect of respectable people.'

"And then if I might quote some lines of my own from my book, "Candlelight," in a tribute to my old high school principal:

> *How many friendships have been made*
> *And proven worth the knowing?*
> *Well, just enough to fill a life*
> *And heart to overflowing.*

"I want to say to my opponent that I congratulate you for having gained the majority of votes of this organization.

"And I want to say to all of you that my regard for the real friendships that exist between us and my joy in living has not been diminished in the least. It's been a wonderful experience, and I thank you from the bottom of my heart."

* * * * * * * * *

The whole thing took about twenty minutes, a far stretch from the two minutes they gave me. When I finished I walked to the back of the platform, out of sight of the audience, to see if the winner would have an acceptance speech.

There was such a relief in getting to say what I'd worked on for days. I kept thinking, "I did it!" I was pleased that I kept my composure, for I can cry pretty easily in emotional situations.

Concession Speech

I was so caught up in these thoughts that I wasn't aware of what all the noise was about. When it finally stopped, someone asked me, "Do you realize this audience gave you a standing ovation for a full five minutes?" Only then did I realize I should have gone back to acknowledge their applause.

As I stepped back on the convention floor, a man met me to say, "I told you it was a waste of time to come to our state, and I am so sorry." I was sincere as I answered, "Believe me, it's all right."

I'd won the regard of our postal family, something to treasure always. That realization put the whole campaign in perspective for me.

For weeks and months, I got up early, stayed up late and traveled mile after lengthy mile in a quest to know and serve our membership well. It required more stamina than I knew I had, but it was the most exciting experience of my entire career.

Chapter 30
Wanderlust

When I retired as postmaster in March, 1986, I had some leave time before the official day. Walter and I drove to Tampa to pick up our grandsons David and Jon and went exploring. We spent our first night in the Everglades at a state park in Flamingo where we saw exotic birds and alligators.

From there we took the beautiful drive through the Keys, and celebrated my retirement day in Key West. We saw a sign with an arrow pointing south and the words: 90 miles to Havana. It brought back memories of another trip when travel to Cuba was normal.

It was 1953 and Walter had won a sales contest with International Harvester refrigeration that paid for a trip – four days in Miami Beach and four more in Havana. We enjoyed the Miami Beach stay before going on to Cuba where we saw our first game of jai alai, toured an alligator farm and saw much of the island.

Wanderlust

The flight to Havana wasn't crowded and the pilots let us come into the cockpit and look down at the blue-green waters of the Atlantic ocean.

While serving in the Marines, Walter saw how different other parts of the world were and wanted to see as much of it as he could. After the children had grown up, we joined a travel club with two other couples. Some of the places we went were Niagra Falls, New York, Canada, Mexico and Nova Scotia. Lobster pots and fishing nets are what I remember most about Nova Scotia. They were everywhere. In the fishing village of Peggy's Cove, identical houses were lined up along the rocky coastline like rows of old coal-camp houses back home.

While Walter, always in search of adventure, set sail on the historic schooner, Bluenose II, I kept my feet on solid ground and browsed the little shops along the inlet. I mailed postcards to the children from Peggy's Point Lighthouse, the only lighthouse post office in North America.

We found Mexico's Yucatan Peninsula to be a land of great contrasts. Our luxurious resort on Cancun's white sand beach seemed world's apart from the rural countryside. Only a few miles inland, pigs and chickens roamed freely on the dirt floors of the thatched huts. Passing closely by one of the open huts, I had a clear view of a rooster eating off the table.

The ancient Mayan civilization, one of the most advanced in the history of the world, is centered on the Yucatan Peninsula. We visited Tulum, the Mayan's only walled city, built on a cliff overlooking the sea. We climbed countless steps to tour the structures and on one of the highest points enjoyed a breathtaking view of the turquoise waters of the Caribbean.

We spent another day touring Chichen Itza, considered the capital of the Mayan empire and home to one of the best-preserved pyramids in the world. Our guide shared some history of the sacrificial practices of the Mayans that later caused me to have nightmares. There are some things I'd rather not know.

Walter retired from his business at age 55 to get an early start on his "One day I'd like to…" list. Even when he was at home with free time, he would take drives over small mountain roads just to see where they led.

He was curious about the geography of the land. After navigating the waters of the huge Mississippi River, he heard you could wade across it at its headwaters and decided to go see. I was still working and couldn't go along, so he took his little dog and drove to Minnesota. Sure enough, the stream was that small.

Twice he and one of his best friends, Jack Branham, and some others took month-long trips to Alaska in his motor home. Listening to their laughter around the dining room table as they planned their itineraries, I suspect the planning was almost as much fun as the expeditions.

Walter was very detail-oriented and worked for weeks rattle-proofing the motor home before their trips. He padded and cushioned everything from the fishing boat strapped on top to the dishes in the cabinet. If a friend came looking for him, I'd say, "He's out there in his playhouse." Sure enough, his friends found him hand-trimming bungee cords or Velcro strips to make sure nothing rattled on the Alaska Highway.

Once he decided he'd like to take the whole family on a vacation. He told me to contact Nancy and Don, Rhonda and Doug, and any of the grandchildren available to go and to find us a place at the beach. I found a five bedroom condo right on the beach. When I told him the price, I knew he thought it was too much, but he didn't say a word, just handed me his credit card. Our son-in-law, Doug, came by a little later and said, "I hear you found a place at the beach."

"Well, yeah," Walter said, "we have a place. I guess it's pretty nice, but I didn't mean to buy the whole east coast." That set the tone for us to laugh through most of that vacation.

Often our vacations were staged around lakes or beaches, but the most special one to me was in the spring of 1972. Rhonda was on spring break from college and we took her to Europe to explore Rome and the southwest coast of Italy. I had read *The Agony and the Ecstacy*, a historical novel by Irving Stone, and it made the paintings and sculptures by Michelangelo so vivid. I never dreamed that I would actually get to see his work.

We made stops in London and Dublin but Rome was our ultimate destination. The Cavalieri Hilton there is situated high atop a hill and offers magnificent panoramic views of the city. On our first evening there, I stepped out on our balcony overlooking the ancient city and was overcome by a sense of awe, wondering how many epic stories had unfolded here through the centuries.

There was little time for reflection with so much to see and do. Walter became fascinated with modern day Rome and sometimes he explored routine life in the city, but he did take time for the most famous landmarks. We tossed coins into the Trevi Fountain and visited the Coliseum where we imagined Gladiators engaged in mortal combat before 50,000 cheering spectators.

I felt I was wrapped in history as we toured the Sistine Chapel and St. Peter's Basilica. We could see reverence in the faces of those who came to kiss the toe of the statue of St. Peter. One of the masterpieces we saw that day, Michelangelo's Pieta, was damaged a few weeks later by a mentally disturbed man wielding a hammer. It was restored and is now protected by bulletproof glass.

One afternoon, Walter persuaded us to break away from our guidebook long enough to appreciate the local flavor. He had scouted his own points of interest that led us to an intersection of busy city streets with no traffic lights or stop signs. He got a big kick out of watching drivers pull into the crossing, honking their horns, waving their fists in the air and yelling phrases we didn't need an interpreter to understand. Sometimes the little cars and scooters darted up on sidewalks and zipped right on by.

Reminders were all around us that the Eternal City is home to regular folks. Laundry hung on clotheslines outside apartment windows; women filled baskets with giant loaves of bread and fresh vegetables from open air markets. Most of the baskets also contained a bouquet of flowers making them appear as important as the food.

Shop owners bargained and haggled over prices and, no matter how busy they were, pulled down the shades and closed their shops for a siesta in mid-afternoon. Back at the hotel, a toga party was the most elaborate event we've ever attended, and perhaps the most fun. Where else would a

horse drawn chariot come racing into the dining room while waiters served wine from goatskin flasks?

On the evening of the party, we returned from sightseeing to find togas folded neatly on our beds. We laughed as we fumbled around trying to figure out which was whose and how they were to be worn. Men were asked to wear sandals, but Walter didn't have any. He went looking in the hotel shops, and we tried not to laugh when he came back with some he said cost as much as an Armani suit.

Another highlight of our trip was a trek to Naples and on to Sorrento where we boarded a hydrofoil to ferry us to the Isle of Capri, one of the places I wanted very much to see. My first glimpse of the island was surreal – a tall jagged mountain jutting straight up out of the Tyrrhenian Sea.

I have a phobia about heights and wasn't prepared for the wild trip up the mountain. Had I known what we were getting into, I'd have missed the excursion entirely for it looked as if no more than a foot separated the wheels of the small bus from the edge of the cliffs that kept getting steeper.

We reached our destination safely, the small village of Anacapri where we enjoyed breathtaking views. The Onassis yacht, Christina, was anchored in the harbor below, dazzling white against the bluest water I've ever seen. I kept wishing our Nancy could be with us to share the scenery and the whole experience, but she was back home expecting our second grandchild.

My nerves had settled by the time we were seated for a candlelight dinner in a rustic little restaurant. Our waiter was no more fluent in English than we were in Italian and, though we weren't quite sure what we ordered, our meal was wonderful.

As a violinist played softly over my shoulder and I listened to the lively conversation between my husband and daughter, my mind wandered back to the small valley of Prater Creek where I was born and the home I loved so much before it fell apart. I remembered climbing to the top of the hill and looking down, wondering what lay beyond the visible stretch. I had no idea the world God created was so big and so varied or that I would be allowed to see so much of it.

As he often did, Walter asked, "Penny for your thoughts?" How could I tell him all the wonder I was feeling? I just smiled, and he seemed to understand that this mountaintop evening was one I would never forget.

Chapter 31

Remembering Walter

Forever and always, it seems, Walter was the central part of my life. When we met in 1941, we were very young, but we were like two magnets drawn to each other. Though teenagers, naive and immature, it didn't take long for us to realize that each would always want to know where the other was. We both dated a few others during our spats and times apart, but we knew they were temporary diversions, and we looked over our shoulders for each other.

By the time we were married, he'd become "the other part" of me, so when he passed away sixty-one years later, I knew I could never be a complete person again in this life. I had to go on breathing and running to and fro, but nothing could ever be the same.

For months I couldn't sleep, even when exhausted. I'd close my eyes, but my ears would ring with the words, "He's gone!" I'd try to think how I could ever sit at that kitchen bar and drink coffee again, or how I could set the dining room table without him in his usual place. It wasn't a lack of faith – I never questioned or doubted God in any way – but for some reason I felt He had tossed me to the crocodiles, and I could feel no comfort.

Mornings had been a favorite time of day, when we made plans, shared thoughts and observations as we lingered over coffee. Then our dinners with family and friends were always special. He had the funniest stories, and we never tired of listening and laughing, even when he told the same ones over.

Not since I was fourteen had he been missing from my life, and I would have to learn how to live without him. I like to dream about him but seldom do, though I can feel and see his presence in the things he left me – our children and grandchildren, trees he planted and the house he loved. I long ago disposed of personal items, except for his watch on the dresser and a favorite jacket in the closet. They just wouldn't go and they take very little room.

Even while grieving, I know he wasn't perfect. We sometimes disagreed, and there were a few full blown arguments, despite dear old Preacher Stratton's advice when he said, "Children, you'll become angry with each other now and then. It's bound to happen, but try not to do it at the same time." But sometimes we did.

Much of grief, at least for me, is regret. It seems the time slipped away so fast, and there were things we might have done differently. I wish I'd been more affectionate. He was very romantic, but it has never been easy for me to show the affection I feel. If we could have a practice run at life, we'd likely all do better on the real thing. I know I would.

Remembering Walter

I never really understood how challenging it was to make a living and build a secure future. From the time I was old enough, I loved working, and continue to, but I had little concept of fiscal management and relied on him for that. When he wanted to discuss financial planning, I was of little help. Now that decisions are mine to make, I appreciate more how he worked at teaching me.

He was a successful businessman with almost no training for it, but probably his greatest ability was his role as father and grandfather. There was nothing our daughters couldn't discuss with him and when one of them needed counseling, he'd ask me to go somewhere and leave him alone with her. He said they had things to talk about, and he didn't want her to feel like she was facing a jury.

In looking back, I guess we made a pretty good team as parents. I'll take some credit for the fact that our girls learned early to balance families, careers and all the demands on their time. They are both excellent cooks and their homes are favorite places where friends and family like to gather.

Like his father, Walter was a wonderful, thoughtful teacher. When the girls came to him for advice, he never tossed out easy answers, but always led them to ask the right questions, to weigh options and carefully consider outcomes. They always knew he was proud of them and believed in their talents and abilities. He taught them to be self-assured, to seek advice when needed but, when it came to making final decisions, to trust their own judgment. His guidance helped them both mature into confident, successful women.

In our marriage, I think we were like so many other couples in taking each other for granted, but unlike many, our interests and hobbies often took us in different directions. He was an avid fisherman and had buddies for that along with business associates, while I had the postal family, church friends and shopping buddies. These all overlapped – his friends and mine – but we did some things separately.

One of the things I miss most now is Walter's leveling influences. If I were upset about something, he let me moan just so long and then he'd clear the air, "I really don't think anything can be all that bad." Then he'd have me laughing at myself. At other times, if I got too carried away about something good, he let me float around a while before bringing me gently back to earth with no effort at all.

After I retired, we had sixteen more years together, and most of those were spent, spring to fall, on houseboats. We enjoyed the time spent at Watts Bar Lake, but the five years we spent on Lake Cumberland were even better. I loved being at the lake with him. Friends and family came often, sometimes staying for several days. The atmosphere was so peaceful, and it was good just being together. Whatever we ate tasted better as we watched the ducks swim or the fish

jump. The area was a natural habitat for several species of wildlife and he had an interest in them all.

We had an ideal dock space at Burnside, a corner spot where the neighbors passed by frequently and became friends. Through the years he became a bit of a legend there on the dock. Some called him Mayor. Others called him Admiral because of his nautical fleet double parked in the adjacent slips. Besides the seventy-foot houseboat we lived on, we had a runabout so the kids could ski, a fishing boat, and a cabin cruiser to accommodate extra guests. He kept a fishing line out where he could watch it from his chair on the front deck. When a neighbor passed by and asked, "Catching anything?" he'd laugh and say, "I hope not," meaning he didn't want to get up to reel it in.

I teach a Sunday School class, and our church is so small there's a shortage of substitutes. So on Saturday evenings, I'd drive home, and back to the lake on Sunday afternoon. It was a 300 mile round trip, and he really wanted me with him. I regret any time I spent away from him, but I was committed to both him and the church and tried to cover both.

When we closed the boat for the winter in 2000, Walter realized the care of it required more energy than he had and we put it up for sale. It was emotionally difficult – he loved it so much – but he could make tough decisions and negotiate almost anything.

Remembering Walter

Anything but the illness. Years of smoking had destroyed his lungs. He was healthy in all other ways, but you have to breathe to live, and he waited too long to give up cigarettes. He had the finest doctors, and they kept him going longer and with a better quality of life than even they thought possible.

That final year was special in so many ways. We spent a lot of time in the kitchen at home and while I cooked or worked at something, he liked to watch and just be with me. He could watch TV from a comfortable bar stool, and we got a lot of bantering in. Sometimes he'd say, "Turn that burner down!" I'd ask, "You like my cooking? That's how I cook!" We thought it was funny. Once I overheard him tell Leigh Ann, "She just knows two settings on the stove – high and higher."

Our disagreements were pretty rare. One was over a shirt. He was to see Dr. Hobbs in Lexington and our friends Don and Helen were planning to have dinner with us there after the appointment. When Walter was dressed to go, I said, "You can't wear that shirt."

He got a stubborn look and said, "Why not? It's a perfectly good shirt and I'm not changing."

"Well, I'm not going with you in that shirt," I said.

"I'll miss you," he replied curtly and was out the door.

I called our friends with some lame excuse about why we had to cancel our dinner plans. Walter was gone just long enough to see his doctor. Later that afternoon Rhonda saw both cars at home and stopped in to see if everything was OK. "I thought you guys were going to Lexington today. What happened?"

We both started telling our sides of the story so she held up a hand and said, "One at a time."

Walter started first. "Your mother just announced that she wasn't going with me if I wore this shirt. So I went without her."

Rhonda looked from him to me, "What's the problem with the shirt?"

"Look!" I said. "You can see his titties!"

Rhonda doubled over with laughter. I tried to explain how the shirt had been perfectly fine when I bought it but now it was worn out and he had several newer ones to choose from, but Rhonda was laughing too hard to care. Walter just shrugged and stretched out for a nap.

When I saw Don again, he asked, "What's the real reason you didn't come with Walter?" and I told him the truth. We got a lot of mileage out of that story.

However he felt physically, Walter never lost his sense of humor. Once we went to Florida to spend Christmas with Nancy's family, and I was bemoaning the fact I'd forgotten some shoes. "Of course you forgot!" he exclaimed, "You only had eighty-six days to get ready."

It was about the first week of February when I needed to run an errand at K-Mart and asked, "Do you want me to pick up anything for you?" He said, "I'll go with you. I want to find you a Valentine card."

"You always spend about five dollars on a card," I said. "Why don't you just give me the money and tell me what you want to say?" He laughed. I knew he liked to buy me beautiful cards for special occasions. I have many I've saved along with love letters written in the 1940's from the South Pacific, Okinawa and China.

Remembering Walter

On Valentine morning, he got up before I did and had coffee made. Beside my cup was a large envelope with my name, and I opened it to find a pretty card and two dollars. When I asked what the money was for, he said, "I couldn't find a card as pretty as I wanted, so I gave you the difference." That was typical Walter.

In late April, a respiratory infection put him into crisis. Rhonda and I rushed him to his doctor who sent him directly to the hospital. The situation was desperate. Nancy caught the first plane she could get out of Tampa and our closest family came to be with us through the night. His fishing buddy and minister friend, Bob Jones, came from Louisville. We did what families do – we huddled to share fear and anxieties, and we agonized and prayed.

He did get to come home and, on the second morning, the sun was shining with the prospects of a beautiful day. Then it happened so suddenly – he was gone. Just as suddenly, the sky turned an ominous black, rain poured and a strong wind blew in, lifting the roof of our patio right off our house. It seemed so fitting that Heaven would acknowledge our bitter pain and unbearable loss.

The grief has been intense, and I will never cease to miss him, but the happiness we shared was for a much longer time. For all our years together, our Guardian Angel was there – not keeping us from all hurts, but helping us through them. If He could deliver a little girl from a swirling, muddy stream, why would I doubt He could lead her to the love of her life? That paper wad, sailing across the classroom, could well have had some guidance.

Because of Walter, my life is richer, fuller and happier than I ever imagined, and we have albums filled with "good time" pictures. Our girls, Nancy and Rhonda, have loving families and both are living their own dreams. There are five grandchildren and five great-grandchildren, with another little girl arriving very soon. They carry our genes, and a part of us will live on through them.

From the time he left me at school in 1944 to become a Marine, whenever we were apart, we were always anxious to get back to each other. Every reunion we ever had was wonderful – and I expect the next to be best of all.

Remembering Walter

Remembered Walk

The holiday is past but I recall
Our walk along the beach, with hand in hand,
The roaring of the waves that rise and fall,
And moonlight gleaming on the whitened sand.

I think about the stars, the clouds of white,
Like puffs of cotton floating on the air,
A gentle ocean breeze that brushed the night
And added to a magic atmosphere.

Our talk about the hopes and dreams we shared,
How each helped make the other's dream complete,
The way we laughed about but little cared
The tide was in and lapping at our feet.

The sand between our toes was left behind,
Just as the scattered gulls along the shore,
But in another place – another time –
We'll walk and love the setting even more.

– from Candlelight

Epilogue

When I retired, I was at loose ends with so little to do. Rhonda's advertising agency was still fairly new, so, eager to help her get started, I began doing her accounting. The work was pleasant and though I called it "helping her," I was much better suited to being needed and busy than I was to being retired. That was twenty-four years ago. I'm still on the job and was long ago made vice president of the company.

I've always enjoyed writing, so for more than fifteen years I wrote columns and feature articles for the *Appalachian News-Express* and the *Floyd County Times*. I did a few articles for the *Lexington Herald-Leader,* but I enjoyed the "Small World" column for the Floyd County paper most of all.

I've written about a few serious causes, but most of the time I did humor and human interest stories about the colorful people we know and love. The column was popular, especially with people who had moved away and enjoyed hearing about people they knew from "back home."

Once a lady called to tell me about some things going on with people who live in her area. I listened, not knowing why she was telling me things about people I hardly knew. Then she explained, "I thought you might like some news for your little strip."

Epilogue

Walter had a wonderful sense of humor and was always sharing stories I could use to make other people laugh. When he passed away in 2002, I took a break and just never got back to it. I had written about so many other people and wanted very much to write about him, but I couldn't.

Before Walter died, Jon had married Marla and they had two little boys, Brian Wade and Carson Walter. Three years later, they had a little girl named Jordan. Leigh Ann has married Michael, and they have Halle Kate, now four. David is married to Emory and they have a two-year-old, John David. His little sister is expected to arrive very soon. Both Candice and Kelly have graduated from college, but neither is married.

Epilogue

I'm now eighty-four years old, and writing this account has been like living my life over again. Some things that I'd forgotten became plain as day when I concentrated on the different eras.

I've had some good laughs as I remembered some events and more than once I had to wipe away a tear. Life has been more rewarding than I ever imagined.

I was always close with my brothers and sisters, and now I have the most loving, caring children – twelve descendants and growing. I also have a circle of friends who enrich my life every day, some nearby and others long distance.

Another important group is my NAPUS family, made up of postmasters and retirees across the nation. The friendships we formed went deeper than our professions and have outlasted our work. We stay in close touch with many and have an e-mail coordinator, Paul Youtsey, in Colorado who serves as "central" and keeps us informed about each other.

There's also the church family I've loved and been a part of for fifty-seven years. I've enjoyed teaching a Sunday School class and serving in other offices, but I never intended to describe any effort on my part to serve the One who gave me life. With every line I wrote, I wanted to tell of the wonderful care He provided me.

I believe He assigned me as a charge for the angels, and they have kept me all this time.

Photo Legend

Page 1	The author at 18 months
Page 5	Sylvia, David, Mama, Graham, Papa
Page 6	Sylvia, Elsie (in back), Mama, Graham, David
Page 11	Aileen, Kenneth (Elsie's child), Jewel
Page 16	Julian (Elsie's child), and Buford
Page 20	Illustration by Sylvia "Memories of Home"
Page 21	Sylvia
Page 27	Aunt Rhoda and Uncle Floyd
Page 32	Buford, Kenneth, Julian
Page 36	Buford, Julian, Aileen, Mama, Kenneth
Page 40	Graham and his dog, Rex
Page 44	Mama and Aileen
Page 50	Buford
Page 57	Walter
Page 60	Charles Spears and Aileen
Page 65	Walter and Aileen
Page 70	Aileen at 15
Page 71	Shelbert Maynard, Don Burke, Oscar Billiter, Walter
Page 73	Georgean
Page 74	Betsy Layne High School Class of 1944
Page 75	Aileen
Page 77	Aileen (#2), Alice Marie (#4), Delilah (#7)
Page 85	Aileen, Walter
Page 89	Jewel
Page 92	Richard and Era Conn Hall (Walter's parents)
Page 93	Aileen with Nancy
Page 97	Aileen
Page 98	Aileen with Nancy Lee
Page 99	Aileen with newborn Rhonda Gale

Page 101	Rhonda and Walter
Page 102	Rhonda and Nancy
Page 105	Nancy and Walter
Page 106	Nancy, Rhonda
Page 111	Nancy, Rhonda
Page 112	Hall Furniture Company
	Nelma Hall, Virgil Carter and Walter
Page 117	Store and apartment in 1957 flood
Page 120	Jonathan, David and Aileen on houseboat
Page 121	Hopkinsville PM H. E. "Bud" Hudson, Governor Bert T. Combs, Louisville PM Bremer Ehrler, Aileen, Lawrenceburg PM W. S. "Dub" Johnson
Page 128	Emmit Conn, John Porter, Walter, Betty Porter, Bebe Conn, Aileen
Page 129	Aileen
Page 131	Walter and Emmit Conn
Page 132	Nancy with her Jeepster
Page 133	Aileen and Nancy
	Front: Walter, Bud Hudson, Aileen, John Mahan, Lib Mahan, Frances Lindsey.
	Back: Fred Lindsey, Delma Smith, Dotty Dawson, Clarice Chambers, Bill Dawson
Page 134	Aileen with Grandson David Walter
Page 138	Clockwise from front: Candice, Leigh Ann, David, Aileen holding Kelly, and Jon
Page 139	Jon, Aileen, David
Page 141	Aileen and Walter with Leigh Ann, Jon and David
Page 143	Kelly Marie
Page 144	Clockwise from front: Jon, Leigh Ann, Aileen, David and Candice
Page 145	Aileen with former BLHS principal D. W. Howard
Page 152	Aileen and Clerk Ganell Clark

Page 153	Div. Mgr. Jim Syers, Texas PM Cecil Stripling, Aileen, Texas PM Jim Wortham, PMG William Bolger
Page 155	Clockwise from front: Jim Chambers, Inspector-in-Charge Eugene Pinson, Mrs. Pinson, Milledge Hart, Clarice Chambers, John Mahan and Aileen
Page 162	Kentucky postmasters in Nashville, Tennessee
Page 163	Aileen
Page 164	Congressman Carl D. Perkins and Aileen
Page 165	Viper PM Jean Hall, Richmond PM Jerry Owens and Aileen
Page 168	Aileen addressing North Carolina convention
Page 169	Aileen and Whitesburg PM R. C. Day, Jr.
Page 170	Aileen and Edward V. "Pete" Dorsey, Sr. Asst. PMG
Page 171	Jean Hall, Aileen, Sylvia Curlee Brown and Delma Smith
	Versailles PM Jack Stumbo and Aileen
Page 172	Aileen and New Orleans PM Jim Gard
Page 174	Aileen delivering concession speech. Walter as part of the audience
Page 180	Aileen and Walter in Havana
Page 181	Walter and Aileen in Nova Scotia
Page 182	Walter and Aileen in Mexico
Page 185	Rhonda, Walter and Aileen at toga party in Rome
Page 186	Toga party in Rome
Page 187	Mountain road on the Isle of Capri
Page 188	Walter
Page 191	Aileen, Walter (holding Zip Code), Nancy and Rhonda
Page 196	Walter
Page 200	(Great-grandchildren) Top: Brian Wade, Carson Walter, Jordan Spradlin Bottom: John David Spradlin, Halle Kate Napier.